CW01624344

LOWELL LIBSON LIMITED

BRITISH ART

3 Clifford Street · London W1S 2LF
+44 (0)20 7734 8686 · pictures@lowell-libson.com
www.lowell-libson.com

28 JUNE – 12 JULY 2013

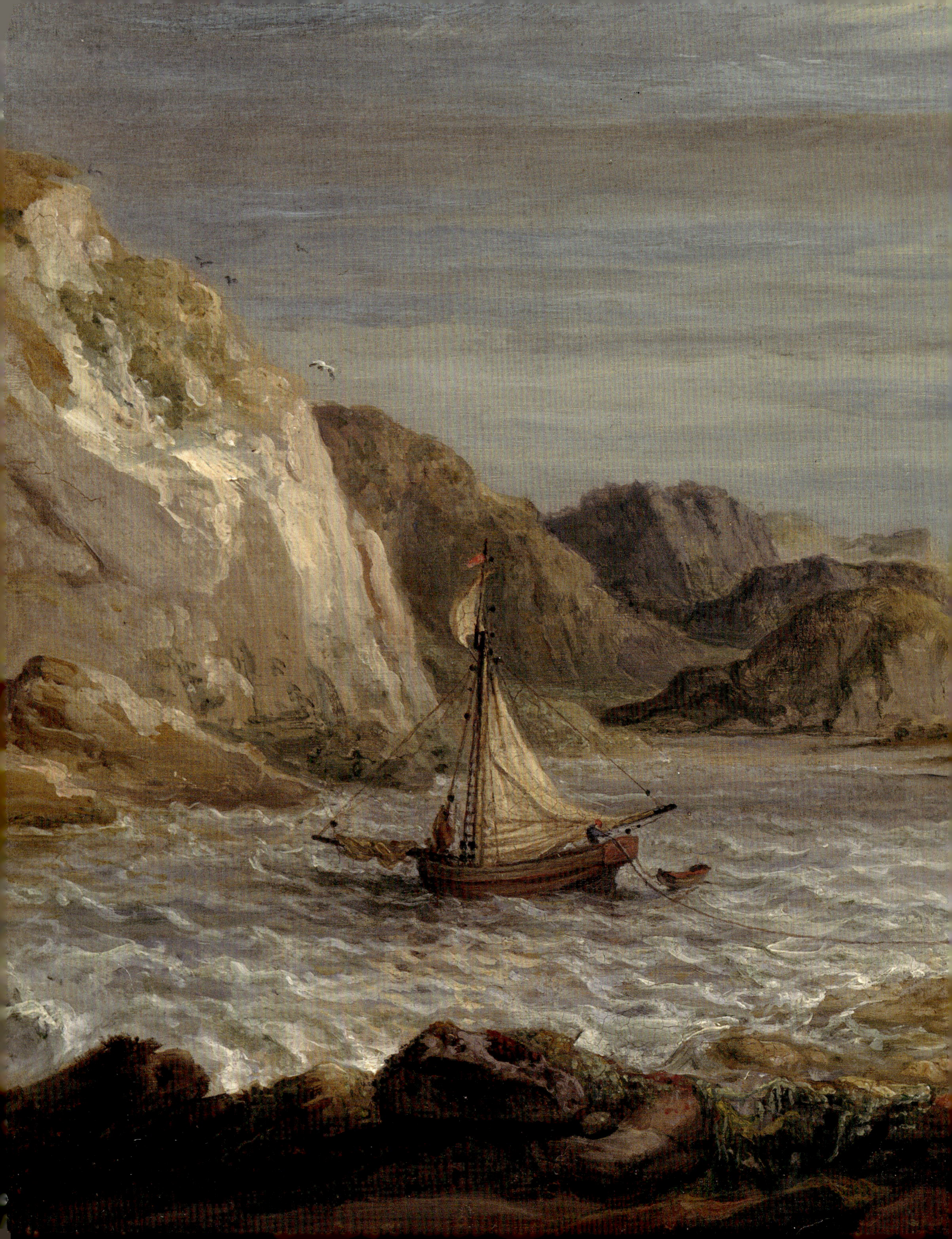

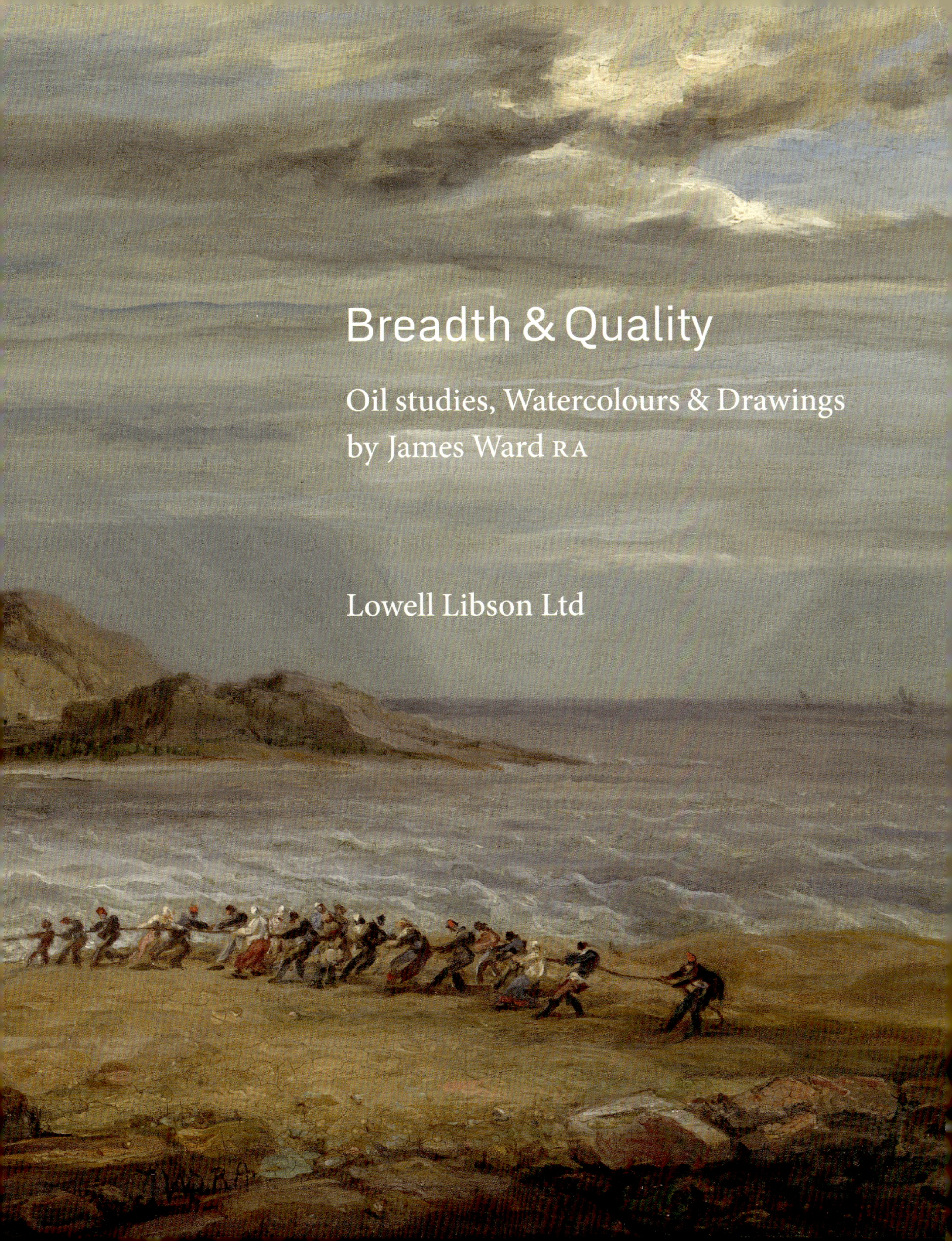

Breadth & Quality

Oil studies, Watercolours & Drawings by James Ward RA

Lowell Libson Ltd

All the works in the catalogue are for sale.
Works executed in oil are sold framed.
Watercolours and drawings are sold mounted but unframed.
Please contact us for further details.

Lowell Libson
lowell@lowell-libson.com

Deborah Greenhalgh
deborah@lowell-libson.com

Jonny Yarker
jonny@lowell-libson.com

LOWELL LIBSON LIMITED
3 Clifford Street · London W1S 2LF
Telephone: +44 (0)20 7734 8686
Fax: +44 (0)20 7734 9997
Email: pictures@lowell-libson.com

Website: www.lowell-libson.com

The gallery generally is open by appointment, Monday to Friday
The entrance is in Old Burlington Street

During this exhibition our opening times will be:
Monday to Friday, 10am–6pm
Saturday 29 June, 10am–5pm
Sunday 30 June, 12am–8pm

GALLERY TALK
Huon Mallalieu will be giving a talk and tour of the exhibition on Tuesday 4 July at 2.30pm

Front cover: detail from cat.82
Back cover: cat.36
Frontispiece: detail from cat.22

Published by Lowell Libson Limited 2013

ISBN 978 0 9563930 6 7

Photography by Rodney Todd White & Son Ltd
Designed by Dalrymple
Typeset in Minion and Embarcadero
Printed in Belgium by DeckersSnoeck

Contents

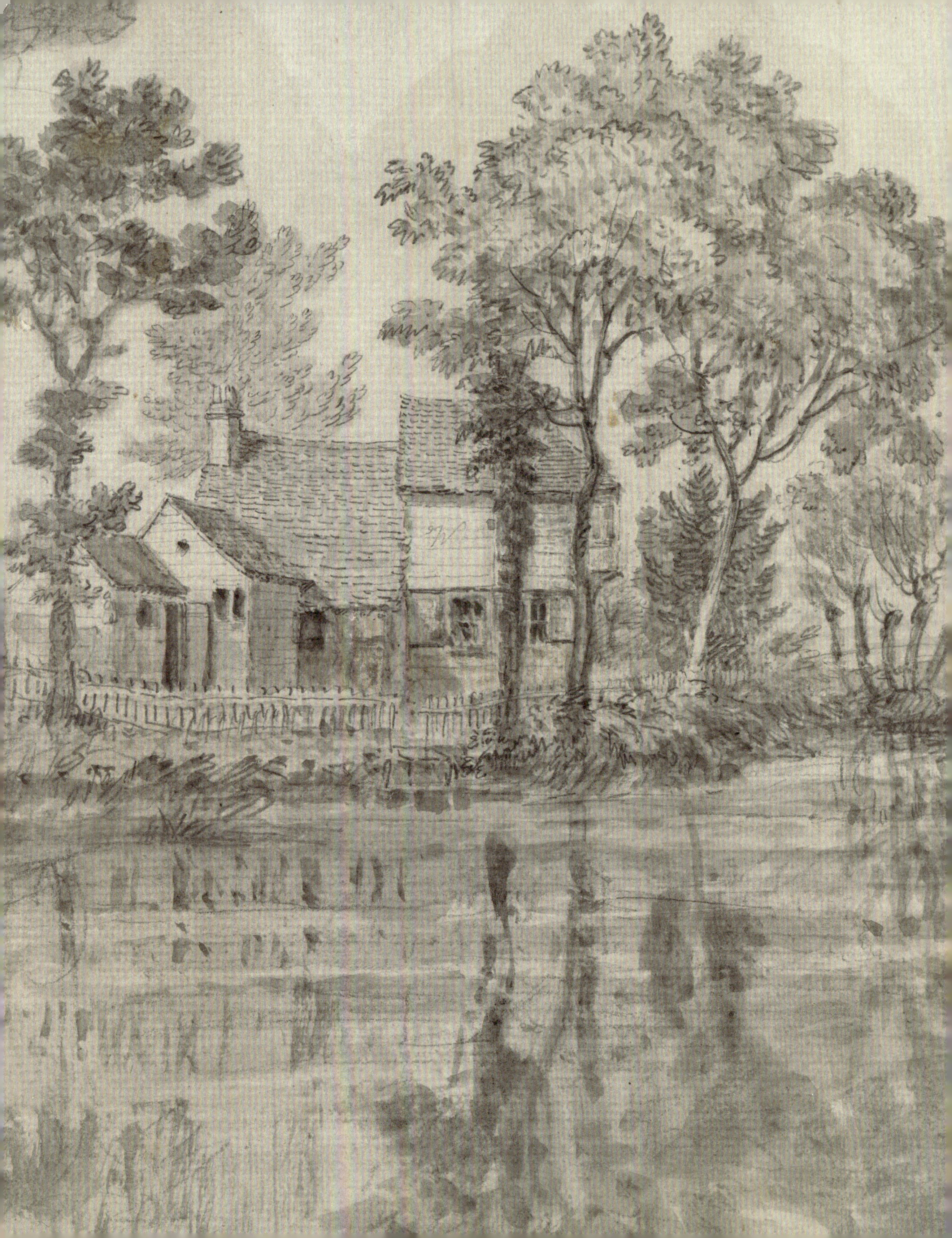

'Breadth in painting is a great quality'

JAMES WARD, 1822

Writing to his son, George, in June, 1847, Robert Ward declared that 'it is well to be abused among the great ones – to be overlooked is to be insignificant …' It has been Ward's fate to be largely overlooked. The recent publication of his papers – carried out by Edward Nygren with the scholarship and care that characterizes the productions of the Walpole Society – together with this exhibition will I hope give us many new insights into the long life and varied work of this complex and productive artist.

Certainly, Ward was a difficult character: manic in his beliefs, depressive and, like so many of the longest lived of his era, neurotically fixated on his health. Self-pity seems to have been his default position. 'Am very ill in spirits through the conflict of sufferings & efforts,' he confided to his journal in February 1818, 'yet Christ in his grace is sufficient for all – see no object to live for the sun to me is gloom and sorrow yet will I trust him. Why shou'd I mind the rage of wicked men or Devils. Lord shew me what is right & keep me in the path …'

His career exemplifies the hard work and precarious life of the moderately successful, jobbing artist with its many difficulties ranging from finding the right subjects to attracting the right customers. Would he have looked with envy on the opulent lifestyle of his friend and neighbour in Newman Street, Benjamin West? With his typically embittered view, Ward linked West's posthumous decline in critical esteem with his own difficulties, remarking that he regarded 'the contemplation of Mr West's fate in union with my own as sufficient to deter any man in his senses from the pursuit of the higher walk of in art in our refined day …' Ward faced and unlike West, with his talent for success, never overcame the fundamental dilemma of the late eighteenth and early nineteenth-century artist: how to reconcile the prevailing, high falutin' academic theory with its premium on history painting – for which there was hardly any demand in England – with the mundane realities of the marketplace. As Joshua Reynolds so painfully admitted in his Third Discourse, 'A man is not weak, though he may not be able to wield the club of Hercules; nor does a man always practice that which he esteems the best; but does that which he can best do.' Ward was no Hercules. But he was a fluid draughtsman, a bold colourist and he looked hard at things. Indeed he seems to have been driven by a powerful sense of curiosity; observing the Papageno-like details of a Cossacks cloak with the same intensity he brought to bear on his lovingly observed drawing of a tree trunk. Perhaps, Ward's main fault, if it is one, is that he ranged across too many genres and media and sometimes veered too close to the descent into downright hackery. He deftly captures the romantic antiquarianism of the post Eglinton Tournament years, and although his history painting lacks conviction, his studies of armour are more than proficient. Ward couldn't be said to make Bonington look like Rubens, but he himself barely reaches the Bonington level. Yet there is real power in his more original works. I am thinking particularly of his magnificent *Bulls Fighting* in the V&A – which plays both to his aspirations to paint history and his skill as an *animalier* – and the beautiful, related watercolour in this exhibition which, despite its small size, conveys a great deal of scale and energy. He is, perhaps, best at England; an England that was being irrevocably transformed during his lifetime, which spanned the Industrial Revolution. The lovingly composed *Mr Rich's cottage* (detail opposite, cat.29) is an idealized meditation on the permanence and tranquility of rural life. Contrast that with the volcanic instability and excitement of *An industrial landscape: a smelting works* (cat.30) a lyrical vision of transformation in which the works of man consume the natural world.

LOYD GROSSMAN

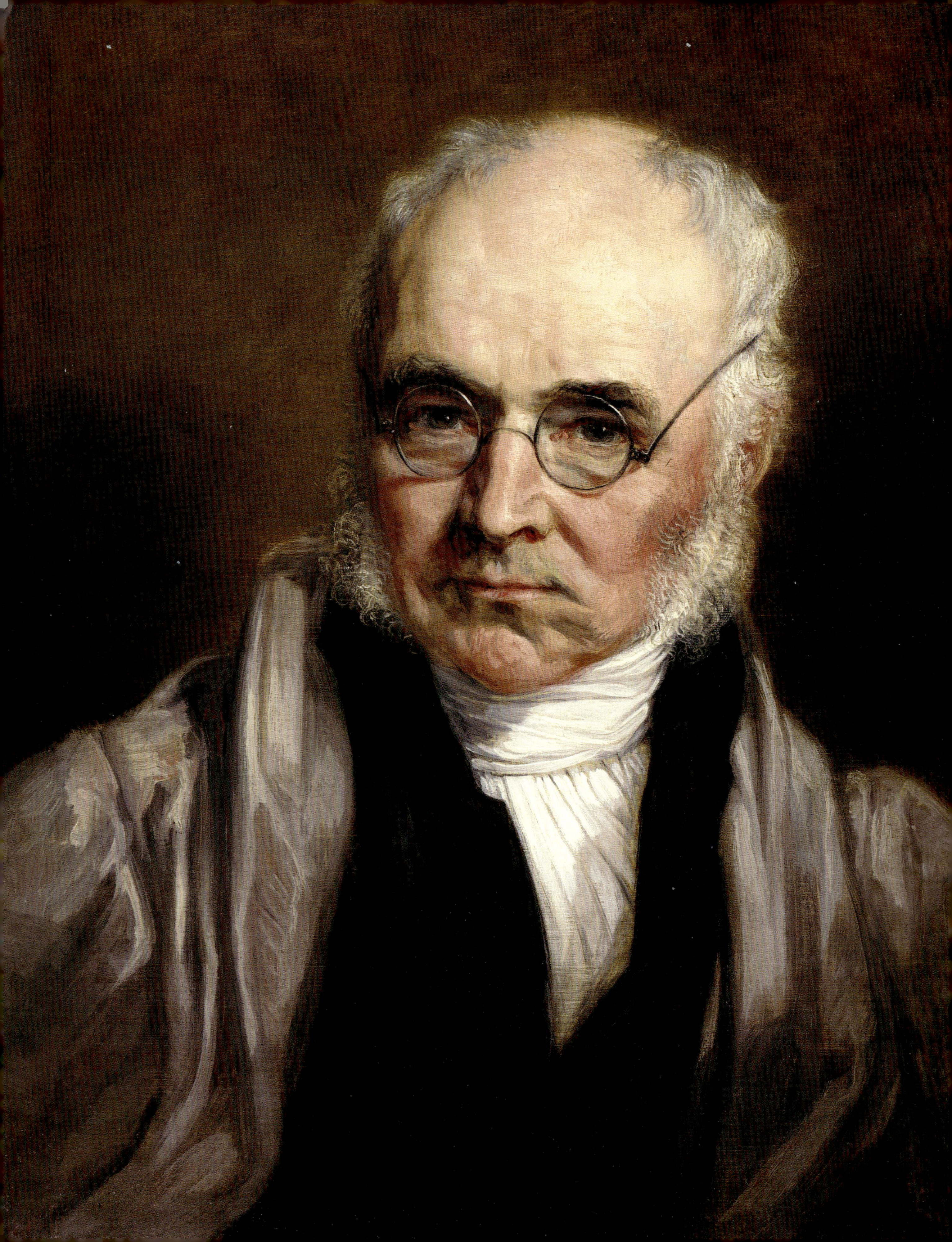

Introduction
James Ward RA 1769–1859

Writing in April 1824 to Sir William Knighton, James Ward observed:

> *As a Painter I have now in my possession studies which I have made from nature & connected with allegory, History, Portrait Landscape, animals & Domestic subject, amounting to five thousand.'*
> (Nygren, 2013, p.169)

This staggering fact, made 35 years before his death, gives an insight into Ward's remarkable productivity as an artist. The group of works assembled for this exhibition aptly demonstrate Ward's remarkable diversity, but they also testify to his incredible facility as a draughtsman. Most revered as the greatest animal artist of the early nineteenth century, this exhibition highlights the range of his achievements and interests including works from nearly all of the areas Ward described to Knighton: 'allegory, history, landscape, animals & Domestic'.

Ward began his professional career as an engraver, initially in the studio of John Raphael Smith and subsequently with his brother William. This enabled him to study at first-hand the work of the leading artists of the day including Gainsborough, Reynolds, Fuseli and West, as well as the works of the greatest old masters. Ward worked for the leading dealer and auctioneer, Michael Bryan, engraving several plates of the most celebrated pictures in the Orléans collection. It was this exposure to both contemporary works and paintings of the past which inspired the young Ward to abandon his successful career as a printmaker in favour of becoming a painter.

Ward had missed out on an 'academic' education in the schools of the Royal Academy and several life drawings testify to his lack of comfort in this genre. But his powers of observation were honed by his work as an engraver and supplemented by anatomy lessons and drawing from antique sculpture. His earliest works were indebted in style to his brother-in-law George Morland, but in 1803 he saw Rubens's *Château de Steen* (National Gallery, London). The picture had recently been acquired by Sir George Beaumont and Ward's work developed a painterly grandeur and rich colourism as a result. Ward was made an Associate of the Royal Academy in 1807 and a full member in 1811.

At the turn of the century Ward created a series of animal portraits for the Board of Agriculture which set out to record the various breeds of livestock in Britain; the compositions were then to be engraved by Boydell. Tireless in his efforts to gather information on British livestock, Ward travelled extensively throughout England. In the process he executed a large body of drawings that he utilized throughout his long life. Ward's imagination as a draughtsman was fuelled by travel to spectacular sublime and romantic landscapes as well as journeys to visit patrons and family. Ward's surviving account book reveals that although he occasionally sold his studies – often for handsome amounts of money, the majority he retained as a vital archive for use in creating paintings, sometimes decades later.

Despite receiving recognition as an outstanding animal painter Ward told the diarist Joseph Farington that he did not '*wish to be admitted to the Academy as a Horse-Painter*' (Farington, *Diary*, 20 June 1811). This reflected a general dissatisfaction with being considered an animal painter, a lower form of art according to the dictates of the times than historical or allegorical painting. Despite his failure as an historical painter, Ward ranks among the leading artists of the British Romantic movement, particularly in his depiction of horses and in his rendering of dramatic landscapes. As such his best drawings, in their combination of technical virtuosity and dramatic subject-matter, deserve to be placed alongside comparable Continental works of the period.

James Ward *Self-portrait*, 1834 · oil on panel · 21 × 16½ inches · 533 × 419 mm · National Portrait Gallery, London

I

Landscapes and Nature Studies

Beckett records that when Ward was about five years old he went into the Kent countryside, helping to deliver cider and was overwhelmed by what he saw: '*the effect on my infant mind is beyond description … it appeared as if I had got into heaven itself.*' (Becket, 1995, p.6) Ward fostered a life-long love of rural Britain, agricultural processes and most importantly the landscape.

Between about 1800 and 1806, Ward attended one of the many sketching societies set up by artists in order to provide a forum to meet and draw landscapes and other suitably '*poetick*' subjects in pencil, pen and ink and wash. Ward was a member of the great generation of British landscape painters which included Turner, Constable, Cotman, Varley and Cox. His watercolour studies show his facility in the medium but he was happiest working in pencil, making rapid, energetic studies of views and individual features as he travelled around Britain. Ward kept these numerous on-the-spot sketches and studies in his studio, using them as resources for his exhibition works. Landscape is a major component of Ward's greatest works such as his *Gordale Scar* of 1814 (Tate). He appreciated the romantic potential of the British landscape, perfectly represented by his atmospheric vision of *Inversnaid* (cat.17) or the fine early study for his view of *Tintern Abbey* (cat.5), whilst also revelling in the simple picturesque appeal of dilapidated rural dwellings. Perhaps the most remarkable pictures in this exhibition include the wonderfully fluid oil sketches of a *Smelting works* (cat.30) and the *Wire Mill* (cat.7), unusual essays in the sublime qualities of industrial processes.

1 OWEN GLENDOWER'S PARLIAMENT HOUSE, NORTH WALES, AS IN THE YEAR 1802

Oil on panel
7⅜ × 9¾ inches · 188 × 247 mm
Branded *IWRA* on verso

LITERATURE: Nygren, 1976, p. 249, repr. fig. 274

A painting of this title was exhibited at the Royal Academy in 1849 (no. 558) and Nygren has recently suggested that it is likely that our small panel may actually be the picture shown at the RA as Ward frequently exhibited works executed on this scale and degree of finish.

Owen Glendower (also known as Owain Glyndwr, or Owain Ap Gruffudd), born *c.*1354, was the last to claim the title of an independent prince of Wales and whose unsuccessful rebellion against England was the last major Welsh attempt to throw off English rule.

A descendant of the princes of Powys, Glendower inherited several manors in northern Wales. He studied law in London and then served with the forces of Henry Bolingbroke, an opponent of King Richard II and afterward King Henry IV. When he returned to Wales, he found that England's oppressive rule had crippled the Welsh economy and aroused popular resentment. In September 1400, a year after Bolingbroke usurped the throne, Glendower's violent feud with a neighbour, Lord Grey of Ruthin, touched off an uprising in northern Wales. The insurgency quickly became a national struggle for Welsh independence. Glendower formed an alliance with Henry's most powerful opponents, and by 1404 he had control of most of Wales. Styling himself Prince of Wales, he established an independent Welsh Parliament at Machynlleth and began to formulate his own foreign and ecclesiasticaly policies. In 1405, however, the tide of battle turned against him. He was twice defeated by Henry IV's son, Prince Henry (later King Henry V), and his allies in England were crushed. Reinforcements sent by France could not save his cause. By 1408–09 Prince Henry had captured Glendower's main strongholds, but the rebel was active in guerrilla fighting as late as 1412. He died *c.*1416 and was to become a national hero especially upon the resurgence of Welsh nationalism in the 19th and 20th centuries.

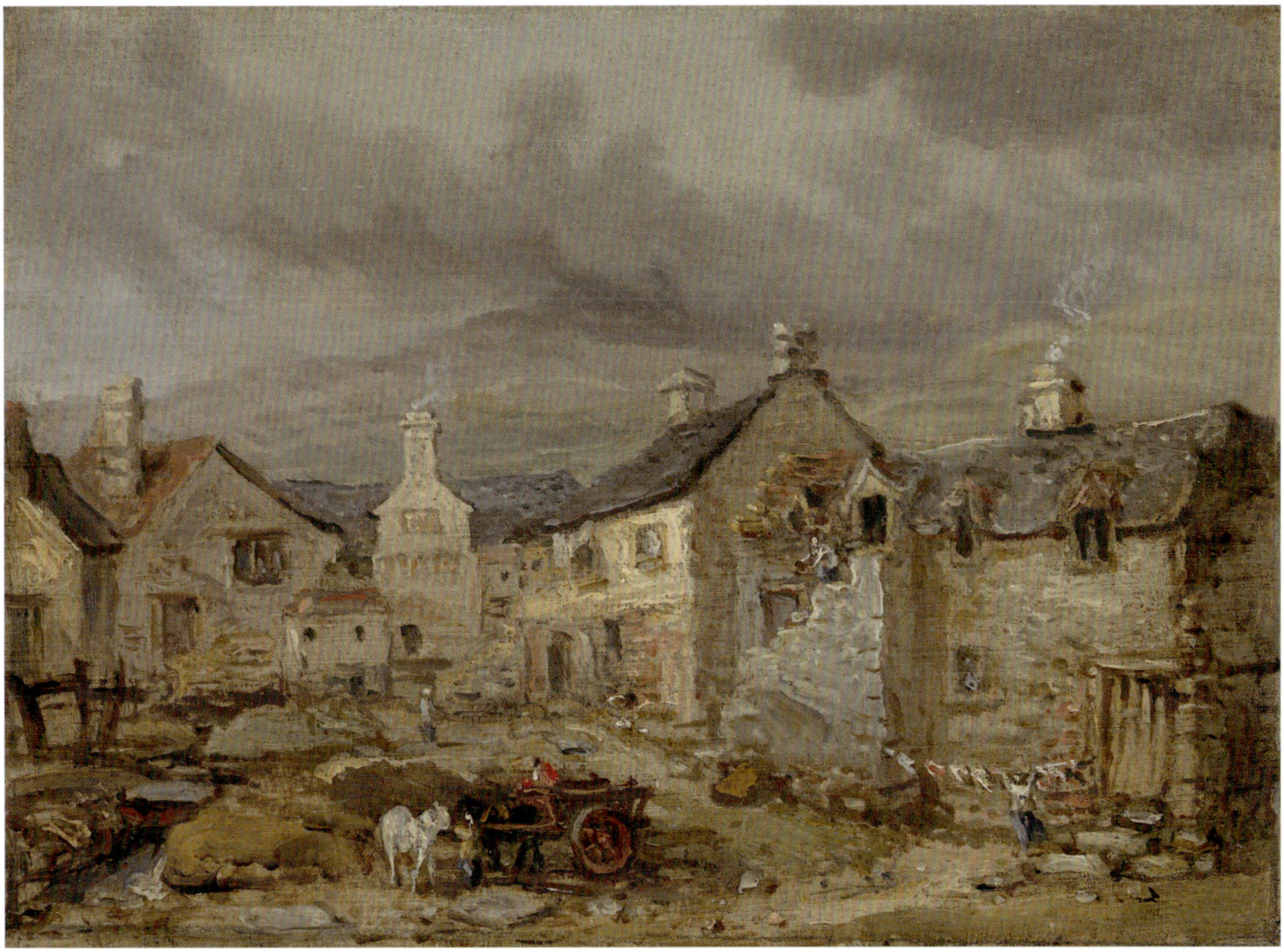

2 A MILL IN WALES

Pencil · 15 × 21½ inches · 381 × 551 mm
Signed *JWD RA* and annotated in shorthand
Drawn in 1807

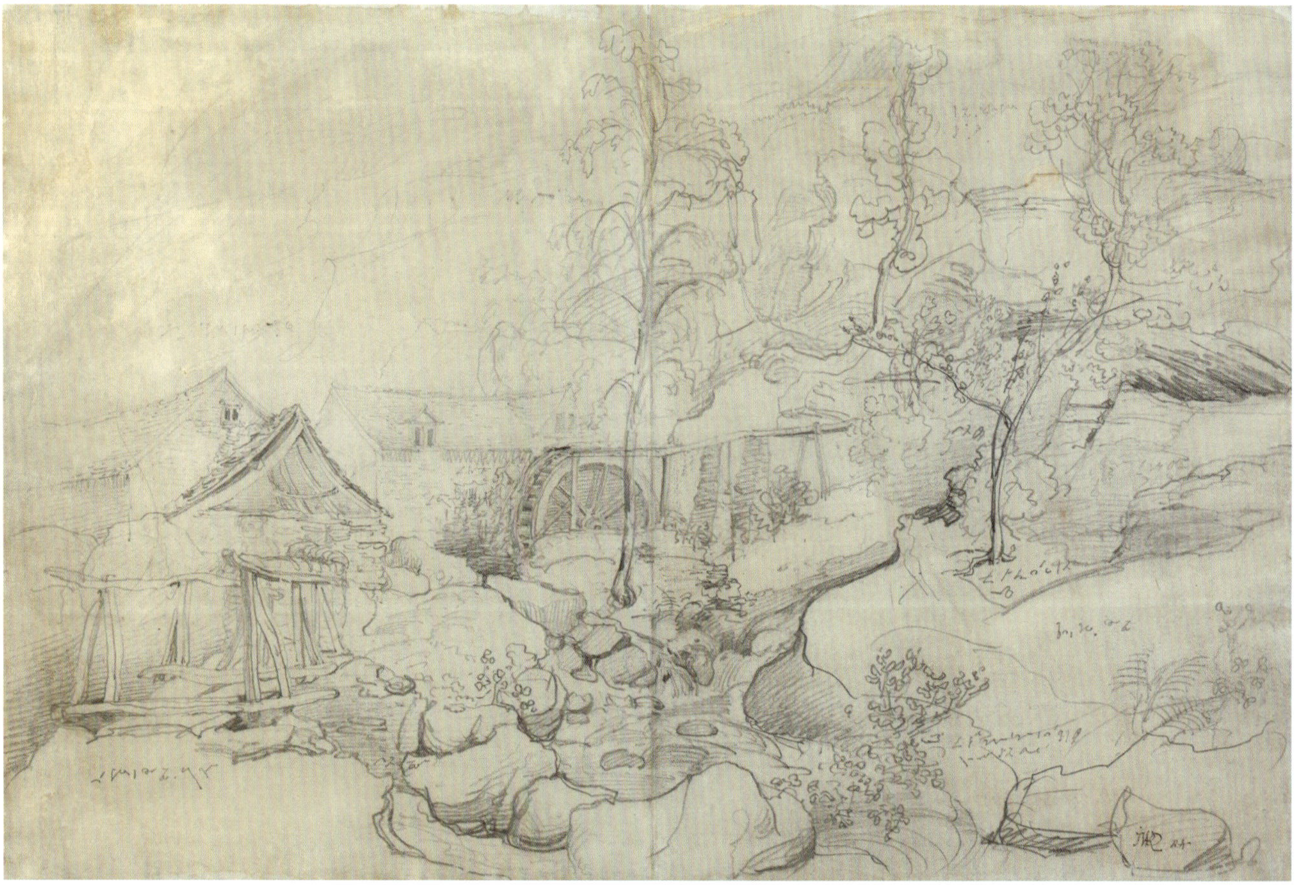

Writing to Thomas Myers in 1833, Ward noted: 'The sketches made in Wales were for the most part pencil sketches; what I would call Gently Lady drawings and done with a sort of headlong pursuit of my object at the expence [sic]of a persever – ing evasion of every introduction to society' (Nygren, 2013, pp.188–189). This remarkably fluent and assured study is far from the standard picturesque views of Wales which Ward characterized as 'Gently Lady drawings', it instead shows his fascination with the rugged landscape and rural industry. Mills were a favourite subject for Ward and he exhibited a painting entitled *A Mill in Wales* at the Royal Academy in 1847 (283), the picture which shows a similar interest for the Mill buildings and its place in the landscape is now in the National Library of Wales.

3 A WATERFALL, WALES

Pencil · 10 × 14½ inches · 244 × 367 mm
Signed JWD RA and extensively inscribed in shorthand

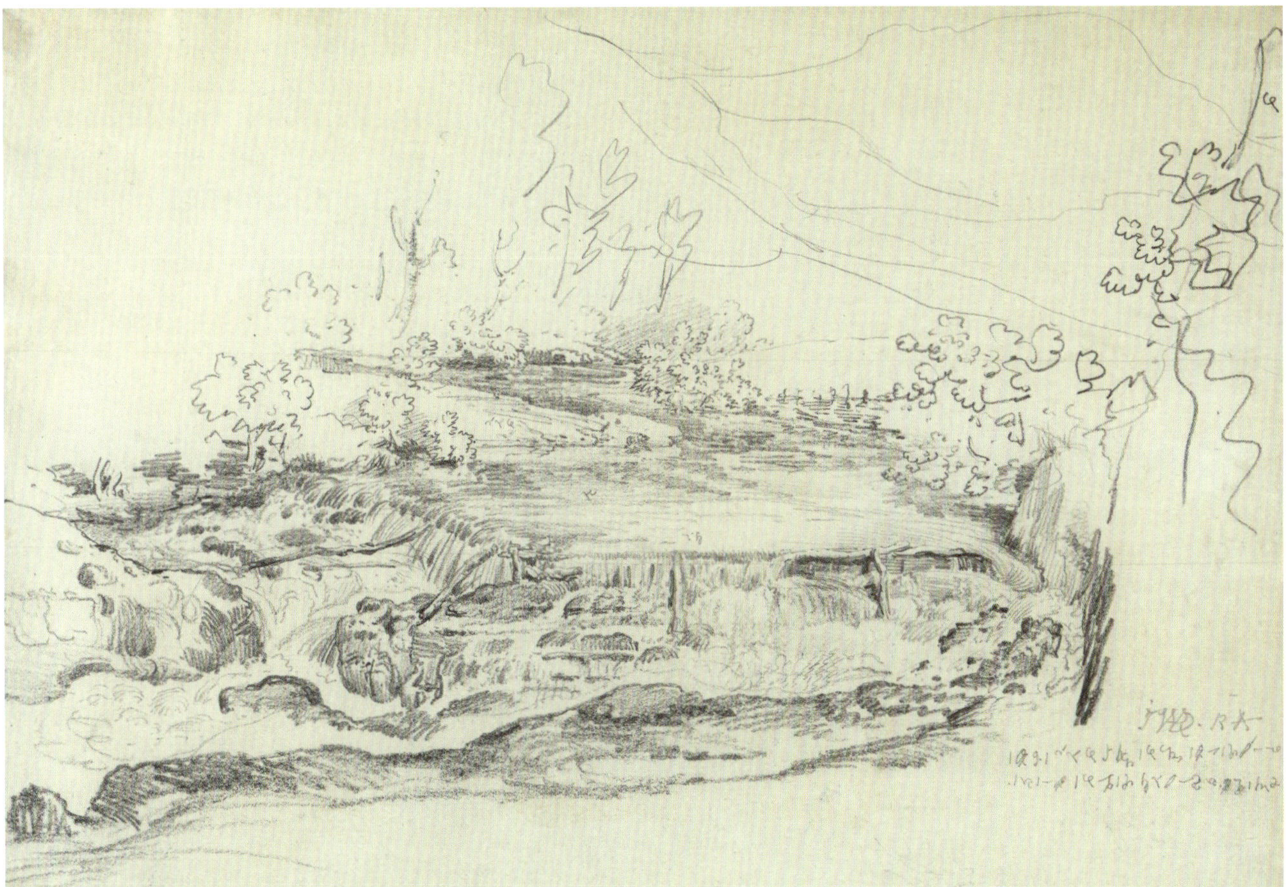

Ward's fascination with the power of nature saw him depict a number of waterfalls in Wales and Scotland. Early in his career, Ward had copied Thomas Girtin's *Cayne Waterfall near Dolgellau, North Wales* (now in the British Museum). Covered in Ward's distinctive shorthand, mostly notes on colour, the present sheet was undoubtedly intended for use in his studio.

4 COTTAGE IN WALES

Pencil · 4⅞ × 7¾ inches · 123 × 200 mm
Signed *JW* and inscribed *Wales*

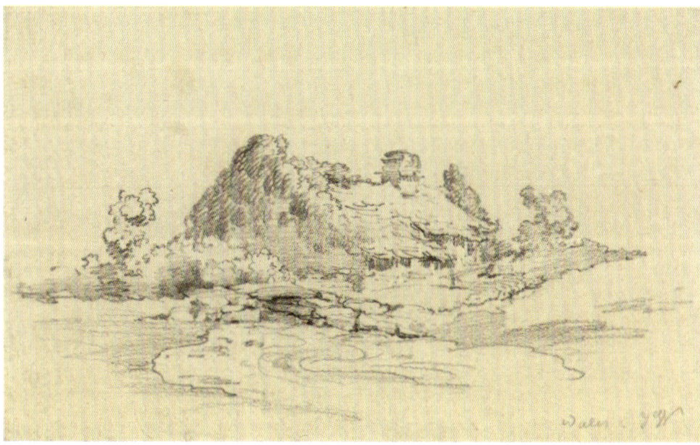

This drawing was executed on the spot during one of Ward's visits to Wales either in 1802 or 1807. Ward must have taken enormous pleasure in the way that this cottage was almost being reclaimed by nature.

5 TINTERN ABBEY, A STUDY FROM THE WEST SIDE

Pencil · 7¼ × 5 inches · 184 × 127 mm
Signed *JW*, inscribed *West Side Tintern* and variously inscribed in shorthand

Tintern Abbey was a site of perpetual fascination to painters and poets during the first half of the nineteenth century. The ruins were made famous by William Wordsworth, whose poem *Lines Written a few miles above Tintern Abbey* was published in 1798. Ward's account book records that he made a 'Drawing and Sketch of Tintern Abbey' in 1814 for his friend Charles Daw (Nygren, 2013, p.114). The present study was possibly used by Ward for *Tintern Abbey*, a painting Ward exhibited at the British Institution in 1838 (471) which is now in the collection of The University of Michigan Museum of Art. Comparison with the finished picture perfectly illustrates the way Ward translated his initial studies into grand Romantic conceptions.

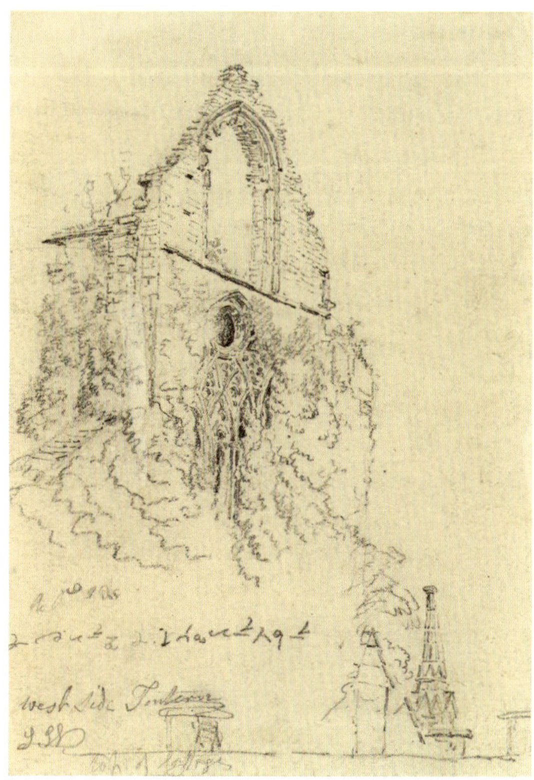

6 TINTERN ABBEY FROM THE SOUTH

Pencil · 5⅛ × 10⅜ inches · 130 × 263 mm
Signed *JW*, also inscribed *Tintern*

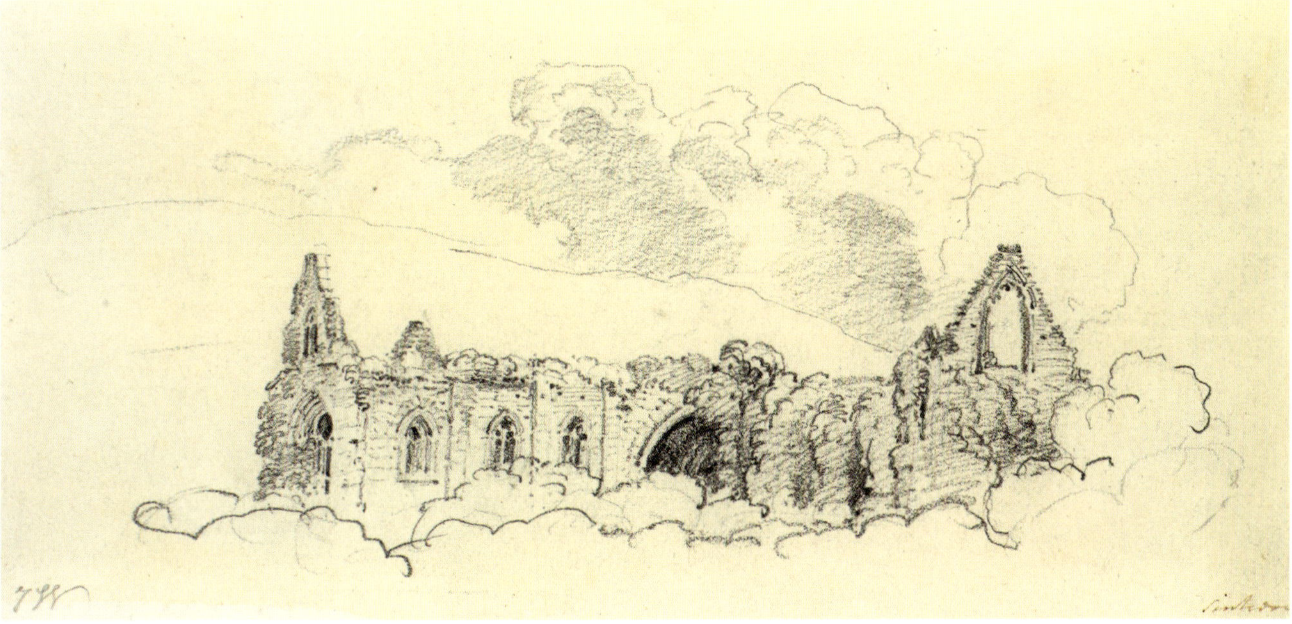

A study of the famous profile of Tintern Abbey, the great ruined Cistercian Abbey in the Wye valley. Popular with both poets and painters, it became one of the iconic sites of European Romanticism. As early as 1782 William Gilpin described the Abbey as: 'A very inchanting [sic] piece of ruin. Nature has now made it her own. Time has worn off all traces of the rule: it has blunted the sharp edges of the chisel; and broken the regularity of opposing parts'. This pencil study was possibly used some thirty years later by Ward for his painting of the West entrance and window bathed in evening light, which he exhibited at the British Institution in 1838.

7 A STUDY FOR 'TINTERN WIRE MILL'

Oil on panel · 5½ × 8¼ inches · 140 × 210 mm
Branded: *IWRA* on verso

EXHIBITED: London, Plymouth, Newcastle-upon-Tyne, Leeds & Cardiff, Arts Council exhibition, *James Ward 1769–1859*, 1960, no.48.

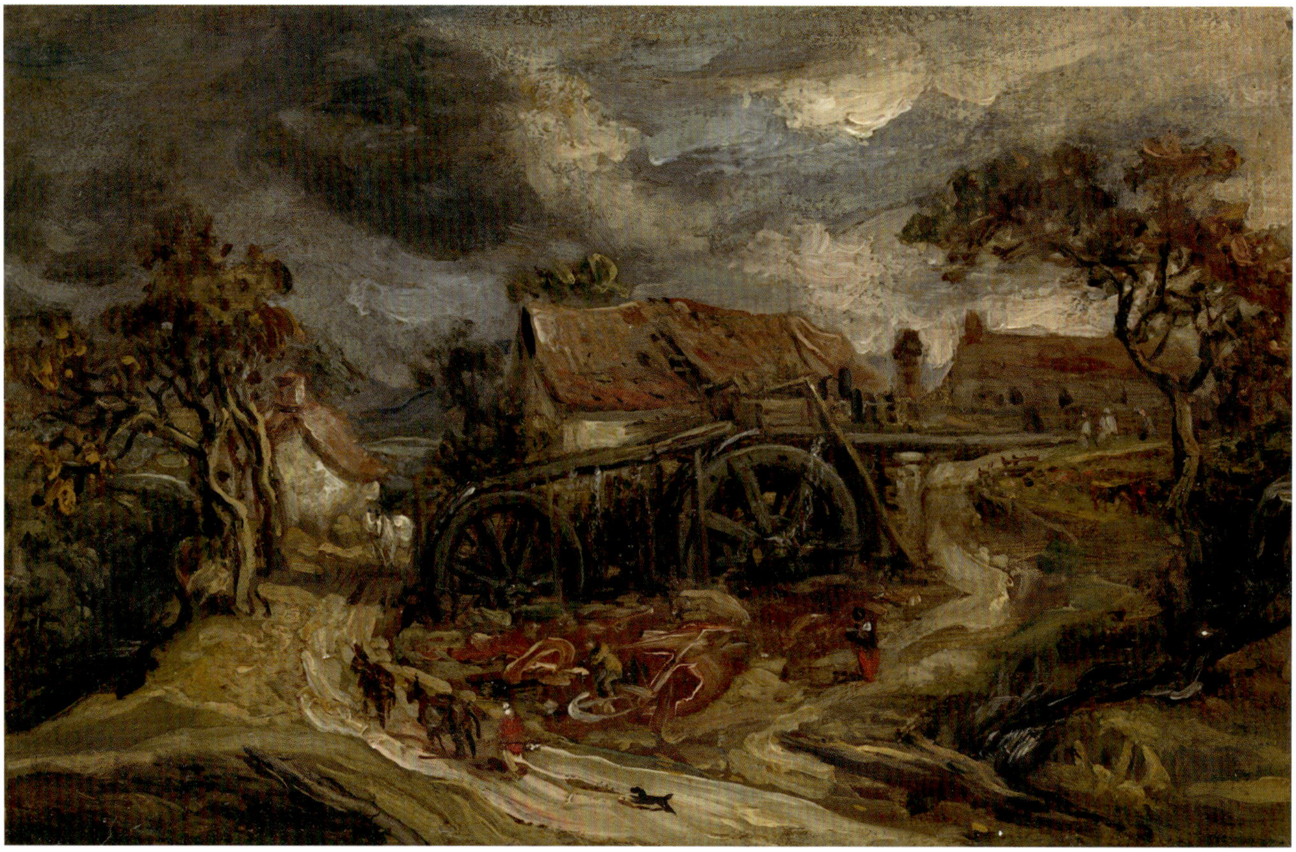

In the 1560s the rich mineral and ore deposits around Tintern were discovered and this, combined with the geography of the area, established one of the largest wire-working industries in Britain. Initially the first metal production in the area was brass but these soon became wireworks, producing a huge range of goods from combs, pins and needles, hooks and eyes to bird cages. Ward has depicted the original mill serving Tintern Abbey. Ward was evidently attracted by the rural industry in its picturesque semi-dilapidation; he returned to the subject periodically throughout his life. As well as the present study, there is an earlier, highly detailed drawing of the same subject, dated 1807 (now in the Yale Center for British Art, New Haven). He exhibited a large-scale painting *Tintern Wire Mill* at the British Institution in 1838 (no.446) as well as *A Mill in Wales* at the Royal Academy in 1847 (no.283). This fluid confident study painted circa 1838 displays his lasting debt to the Dutch landscape masters of the seventeenth century.

8 A THATCHED DWELLING ON THE OUTSKIRTS OF A VILLAGE

Pencil · 7½ × 8¾ inches · 190 × 225mm
Signed *JW* and inscribed *the red of the whole* [?] *& the white to the left above bit of brick under bird cage*

9 A THATCHED COTTAGE

Pencil · 4⅝ × 7 inches · 117 × 178 mm
Signed *JWD RA* and inscribed in shorthand

These characteristic pencil studies are typical of the kind of on-the-spot studies Ward made during his frequent sketching trips around Britain. As his correspondence and diaries make clear, Ward was fascinated by rural life and enchanted by the picturesque qualities of domestic architecture.

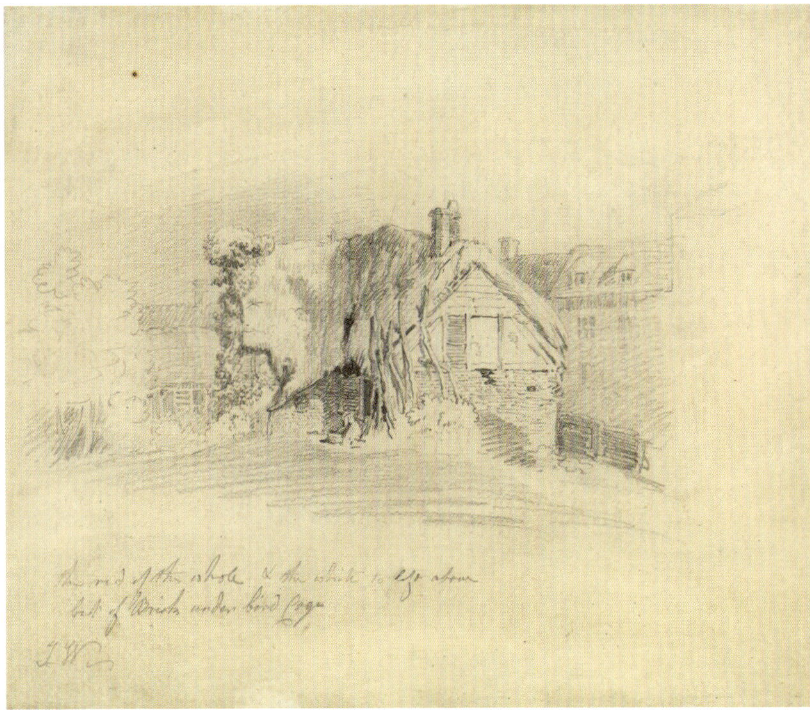

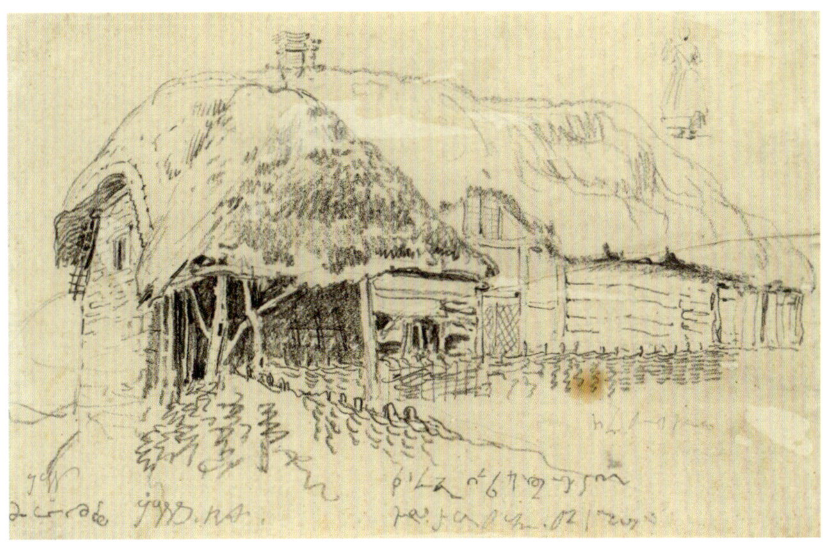

10 A COTTAGE IN HODSON, NEAR CHISELDON, WILTSHIRE

Pencil · 4¼ × 5½ inches · 104 × 140 mm
Signed *JW* and inscribed *Hodson, Chiseldon* and further inscribed with shorthand notes

Like many of his contemporaries Ward took evident delight in ramshackle picturesque architecture and the opportunity they offered to explore contrasting textures and materials. Chiseldon in Wiltshire was the home of Ward's friends Henry Bullock and his wife Arabella, who was rector of Castle Easton and vicar of Chiseldon. There are other drawings by Ward of Chiseldon which are dated August 1822, (see cat.11).

11 CHISELDON MILLS, NEAR MARLBOROUGH, WILTSHIRE

Pen and brown ink and grey wash · 9 × 11⅝ inches · 230 × 295 mm
Signed *JWD RA*, dated *Augst 19th 1822* and inscribed, *sheep wash / Chisseldon [sic] Mills*

COLLECTIONS: Frank Davies; Sydney F. Sabin by 1939; Private collection, UK

Ward made various trips to Wiltshire throughout his career, staying with the various patrons and friends he had in the county. This included Henry Bullock and his wife Arabella Calley who lived in Chiseldon as well as with various members of the Maurice family who were related by marriage to the Bullocks and lived in nearby Marlborough. There was no record of a mill in Chiseldon on any maps from the nineteenth century, there was however, another mill in the parish of Chiseldon, in the neighbouring hamlet of Badbury and it seems likely that Ward here depicts Badbury mill. Another drawing of Chiseldon produced during the same visit to Wiltshire in 1822 is in the Whitworth Art Gallery, Manchester.

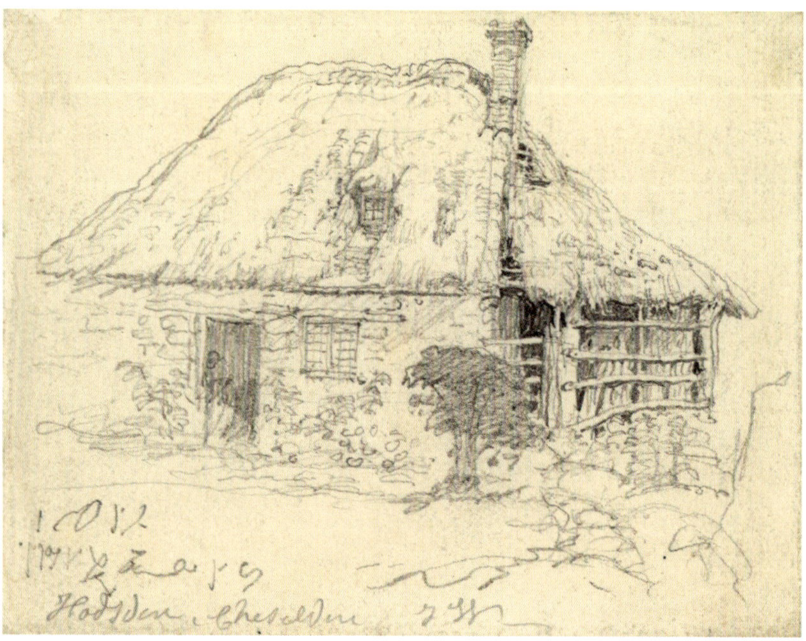

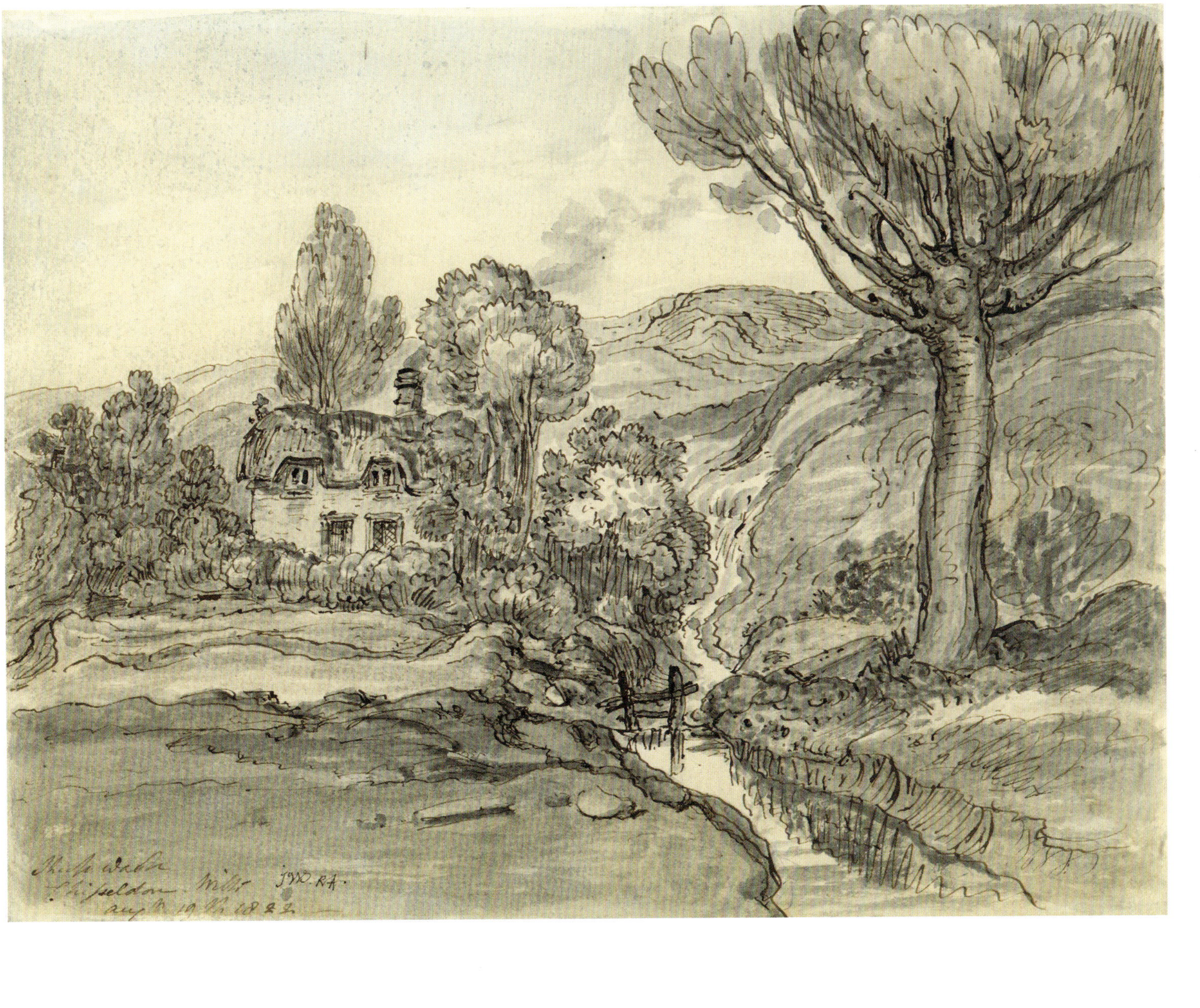
Shipseldon Mills JW. RA.
Aug 19th 1822

12 HARLECH CASTLE

Pencil · 5¾ × 9¾ inches · 146 × 246mm
Signed: *JWD RA*

13 FIGURE ON A BRIDGE WITH A VILLAGE BEYOND

Pen and black and brown ink and grey wash
8¼ × 10½ inches · 210 × 267 mm

COLLECTIONS: Michael Ingram

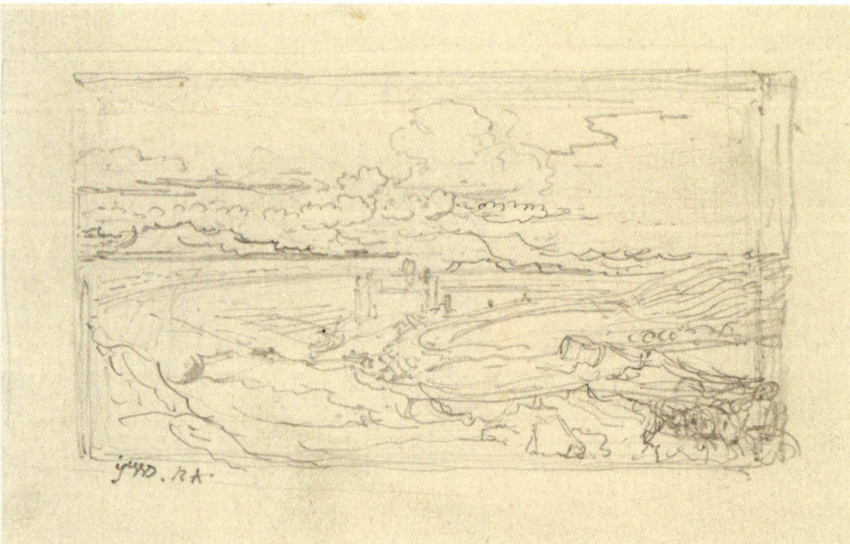

This is a study for the painting *Harlech Castle* which Ward exhibited at the Royal Academy in 1808. The painting was subsequently purchased from Ward for 200 guineas by the Rev. John Ward, a Derbyshire clergyman of distant relationship in 1810 and later passed to the Tate Gallery. The present drawing is closely related to a slightly smaller highly finished watercolour (private collection, UK) which, as in this work, does not include the fallen tree seen in the immediate foreground of the Tate picture. Ward has drawn a frame around the composition, raising the possibility that the present sketch was made after the watercolour, rather than before.

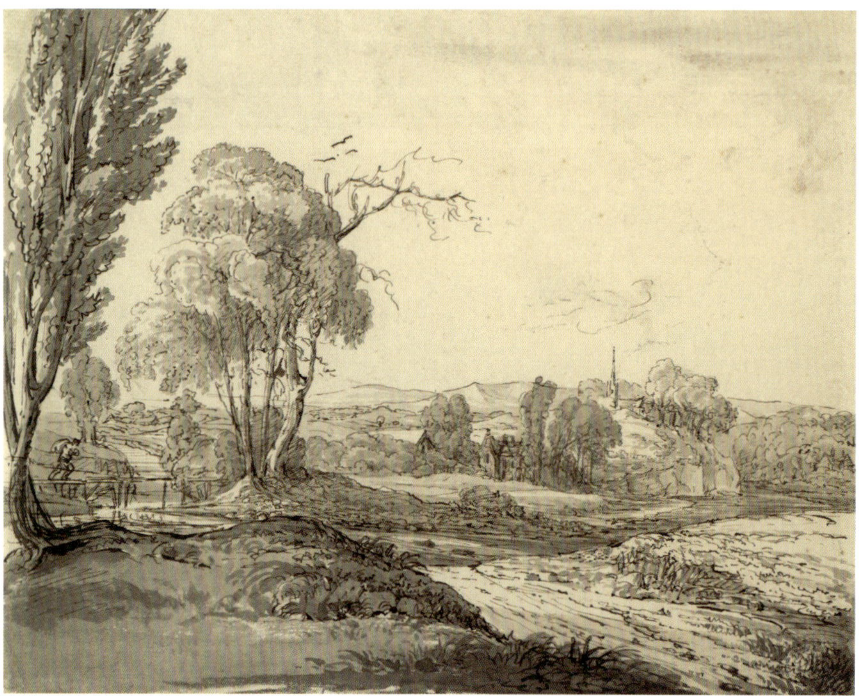

14 DUNSTER CASTLE, SOMERSET

Pencil · 5¼ × 7½ inches · 134 × 192 mm
Signed *JWD RA*, inscribed *Dunster Castle* and also extensively inscribed in shorthand

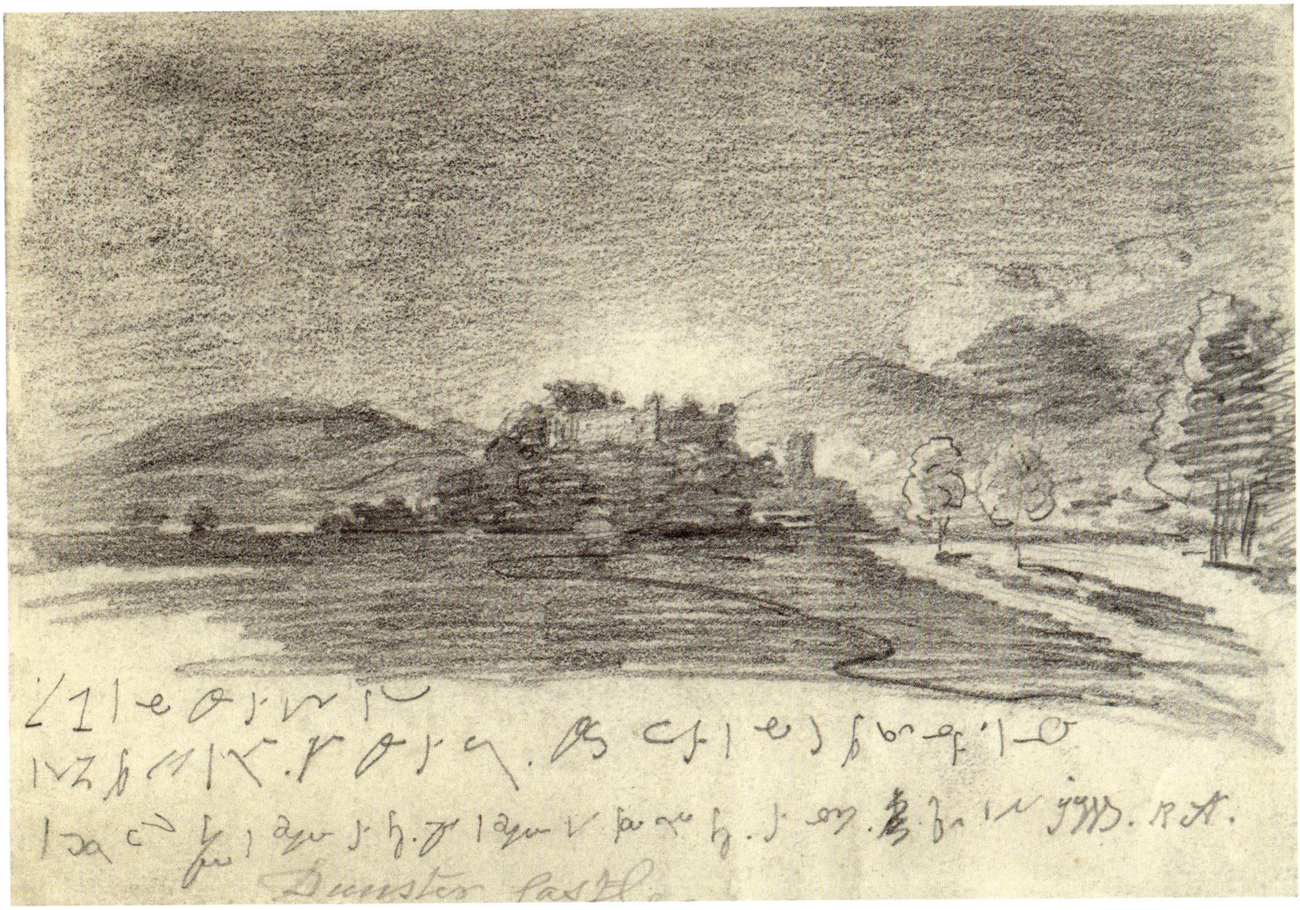

This atmospheric pencil study of the Dunster Castle in Somerset may well relate to a painting of the same subject Ward exhibited in his Newman Street Gallery in 1841. William Holdsworth and William Aldridge invented the shorthand used by Ward and the painter Robert Hills. It was first published in 1766 as: 'Natural Short-hand, wherein the nature of speech and the manner of pronunciation are briefly explained'. Ward principally used it to record colour notes and observations which would be of use to him when working from the sketches back in his studio.

15 LEA CASTLE FROM THE PARK

Drawn in 1814
Pen and black ink
11½ × 183 / 16 inches · 292 × 462 mm

COLLECTIONS: John Knight of Wolverley, the builder and owner of Lea Castle; and by descent to; Major E. A. Knight, Wolverley House, 1908; and by descent

John Knight, the nephew of Coplestone Warre Bampfield, was an important landowner in the area around Kidderminster in Worcestershire where his Wolverley and Lea estates were situated. In the early years of the nineteenth century he built the neo-Gothic Lea Castle (now demolished) and it would appear that he commissioned Ward, a number of whose paintings he owned, to make a record of his house. This and the following drawing, are part of a small number of similarly sized sheets, all executed in pen and ink which must have been the result of this commission. A smaller less highly resolved drawing directly related to the present composition was formerly in the collection of Mrs E. M. Ward.

John Knight also commissioned the painting *The Pool of Bethesda* for Lea Castle (see cat.36)

16 LEA CASTLE FROM THE RIVER STOUR

Pen and black ink
11⅜ × 18 inches · 289 × 457 mm
Signed *JWD RA*, inscribed and dated: *Lea Castle August 1814*

COLLECTIONS: John Knight of Wolverley, the builder and owner of Lea Castle; and by descent to; Major E. A. Knight, Wolverley House, 1908; and by descent

John Knight was one of Ward's most important patrons, purchasing and commissioning works of some £400 or more from the artist (Nygren, 2013, p.393). He was a major patron of contemporary art, Governor of the British Institution and appears frequently in Ward's surviving correspondence. This study is one of a number Ward produced of Knight's house and estate, Lea Castle, which he had built on the River Stour. The drawings demonstrate the care and attention Ward lavished on the commission.

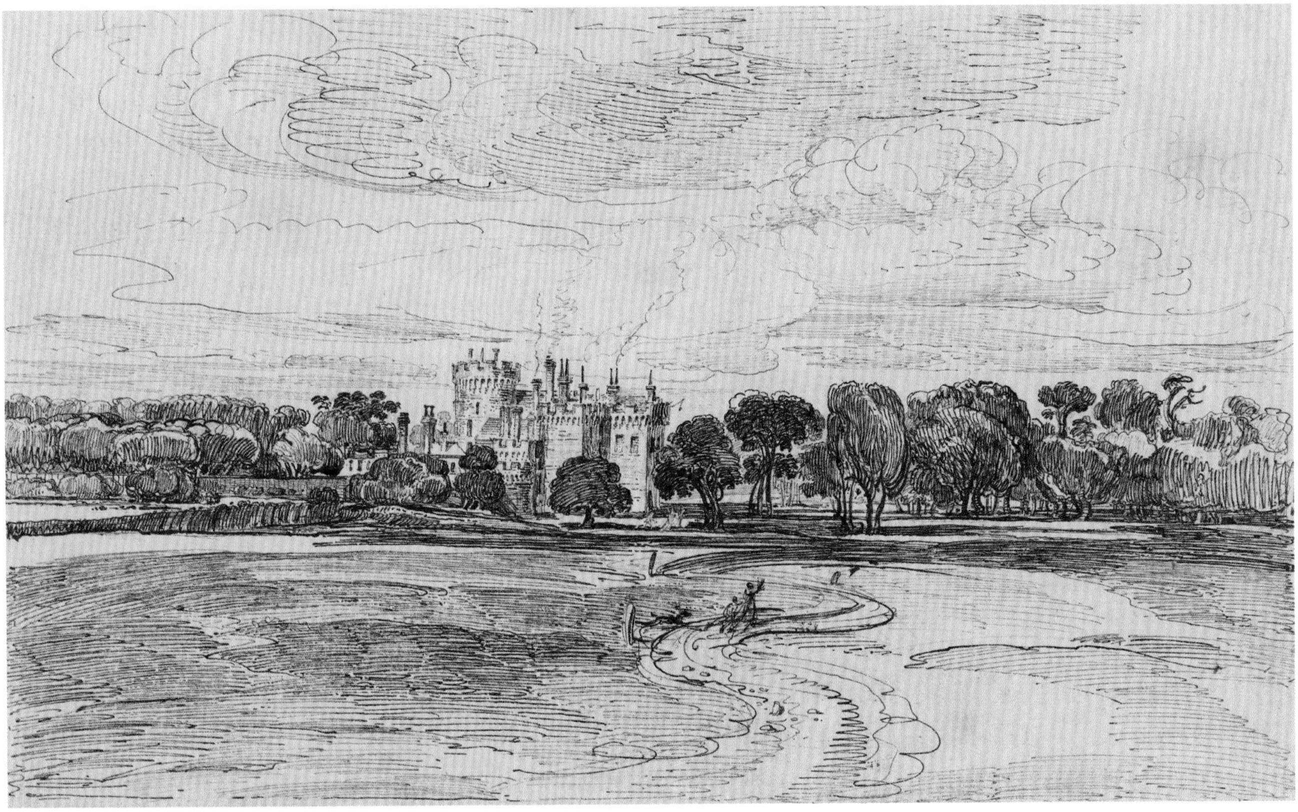

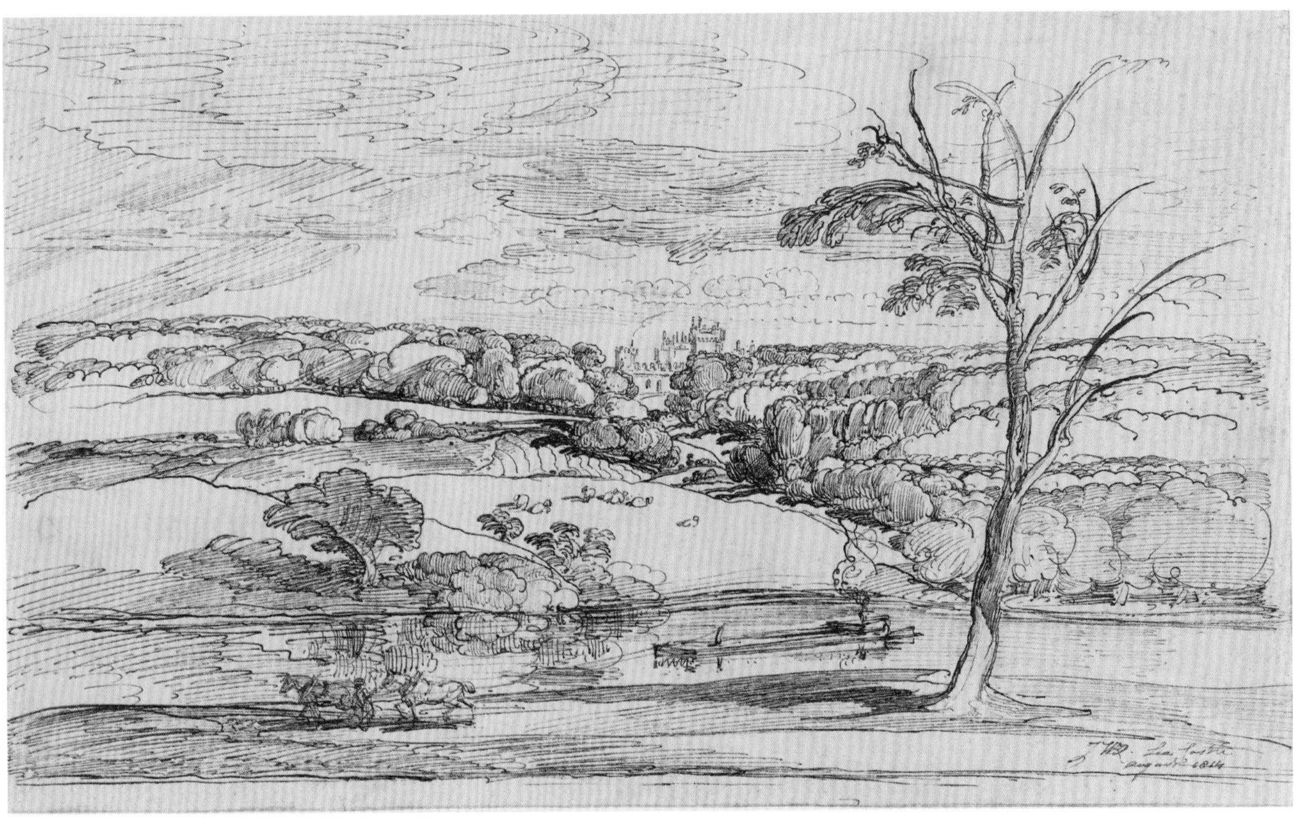

17 INVERSNAID

Grey wash and pencil, heightened with white
9½ × 22¾ inches · 242 × 578 mm, on two joined sheets
Signed *J W RA* and inscribed *Inversnaide Scotland / the old Garrison*

EXHIBITED: London, Plymouth, Newcastle-upon-Tyne, Leeds & Cardiff, Arts Council exhibition, *James Ward 1769–1859*, 1960, no.65

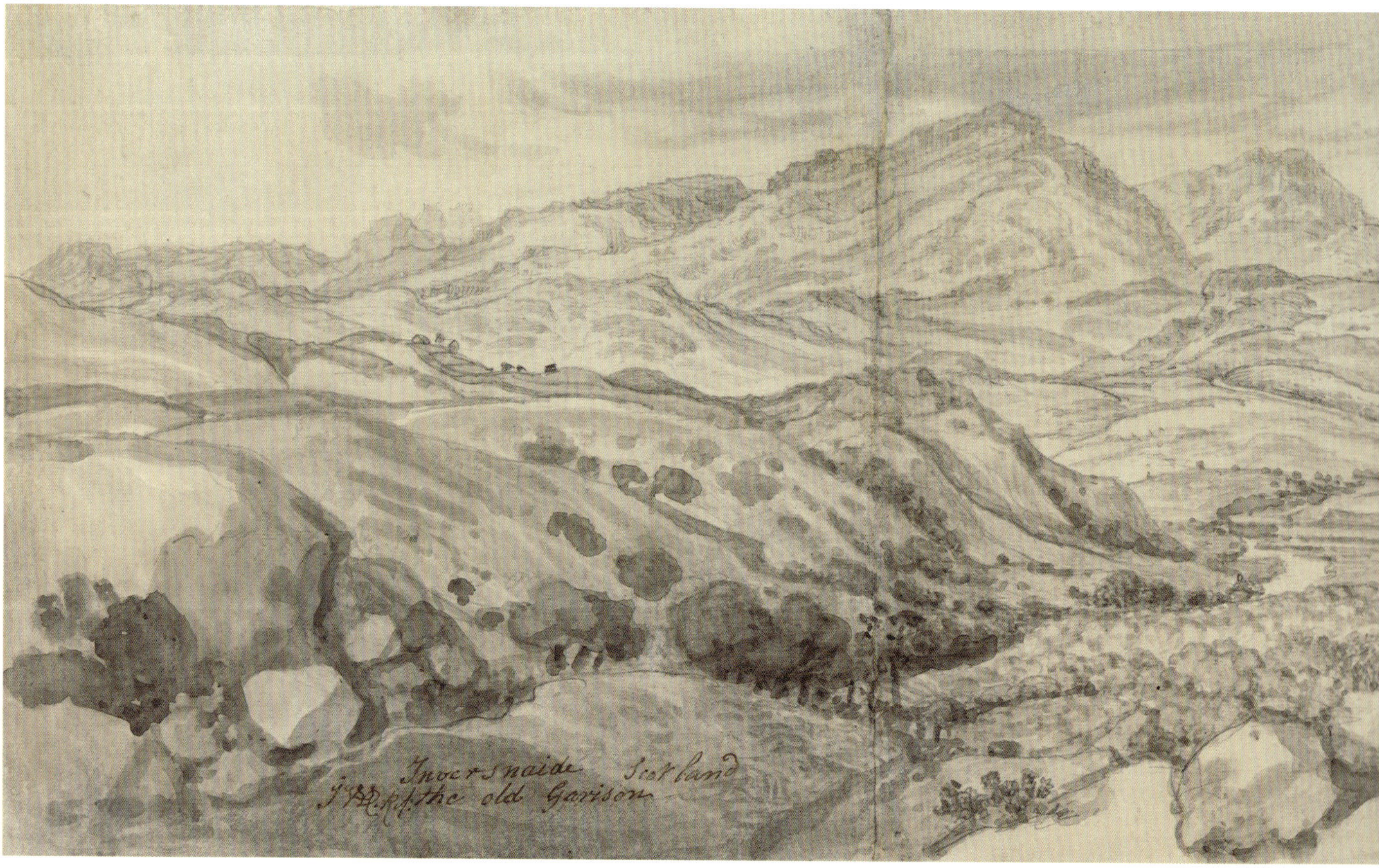

Inversnaid overlooks the pass between Loch Katrine and Loch Lomond and the garrison was built in 1719 in the aftermath of the 1715 Jacobite uprising. Inversnaid was a popular destination for tourists; William and Dorothy Wordsworth in company with Samuel Taylor Coleridge visited the garrison in 1803. A smaller drawing of the present subject was exhibited in the Arts Council's exhibition, dated 23rd August. A number of other works from this trip survive including a drawing of *Loch Lomond looking towards Luss*, dated 21st August and another of a *Mrs McNab of Inversnaid spinning*, dated 24th August.

These studies resulted in a number of exhibition pictures during the 1840s, including *Flocks Coming from the Mountains to a Sheep Fair at Luss, Loch Lomond* exhibited at the British Institution in 1846 (414). The present study is a remarkably bold treatment of the expansive landscape, giving an almost bird's-eye view over the landscape. A similarly expansive Scottish view made on the same trip was formerly in the collection of Charles Ryskamp.

18 NEAR CARNWATH, SCOTLAND

Pen and ink over Pencil · 5⅞ × 9 inches · 150 × 229 mm
Signed *JW* and inscribed *near Carnworth / August* 4, further inscribed in shorthand

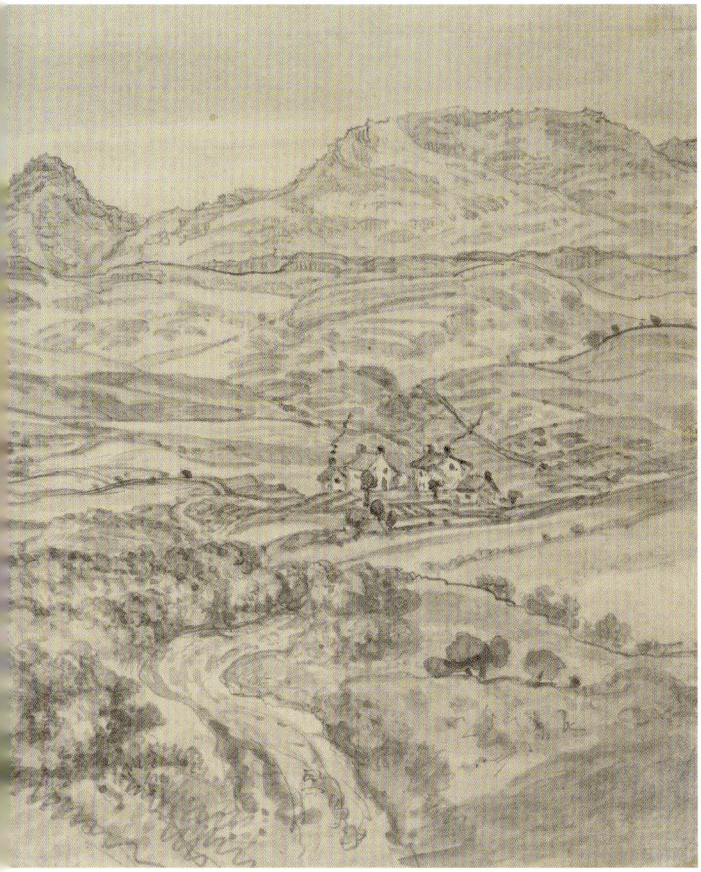

Carnwath is a moorland village on the southern edge of the Pentland Hills of Lanarkshire, Scotland. The village lies about 30 miles south of both Edinburgh and Glasgow which Ward visited in 1805 on his tour of Scotland. The present ink and pencil drawing is a fine fluid study, demonstrating Ward's fascination with the organic patterns of landscape.

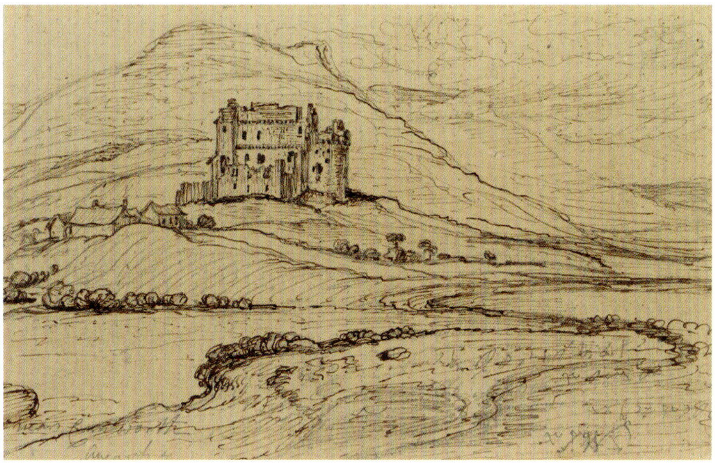

19 LANDSCAPE NEAR LOCH LOMOND WITH WHISKY STILLS IN THE DISTANCE

Pencil and wash
$4\frac{3}{4} \times 9$ inches · 120×228 mm
Signed JWD RA and inscribed *August 23 / Wisky stalors*

20 A DISTANT VIEW OF TUTBURY CASTLE, DERBYSHIRE

Pencil · $4\frac{3}{4} \times 7\frac{3}{4}$ inches · 121×197 mm
Signed *JWD* and inscribed and dated: *Tutbury Castle / Augt 1820*

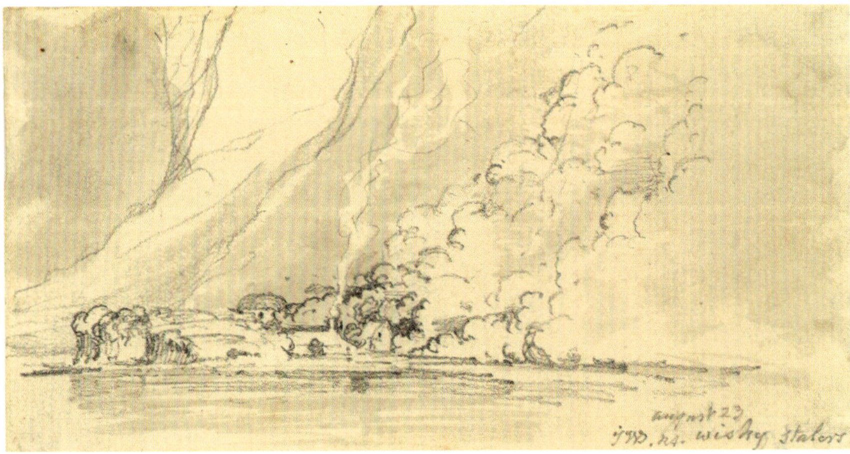

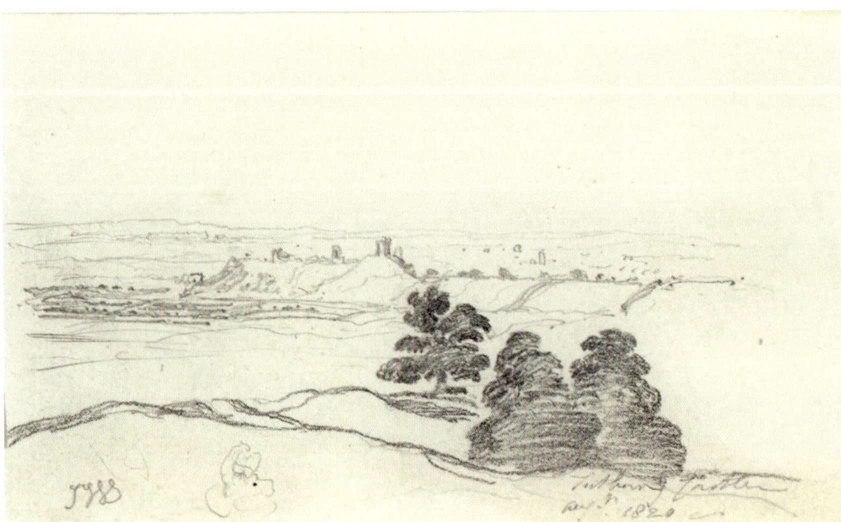

Tutbury Castle, part of the estates of the Duchy of Lancaster, commands extensive views across the plain of the Dove to the Derbyshire hills beyond. Mary Queen of Scots was held prisoner there, complaining bitterly about the cold, decay and damp. This rapid on-the-spot sketch shows Ward's delight in dramatic vistas and expansive landscapes.

21 LANDSCAPE STUDY

Pen and ink
7⅛ × 8¾ inches · 182 × 223 mm
Signed: *JW*

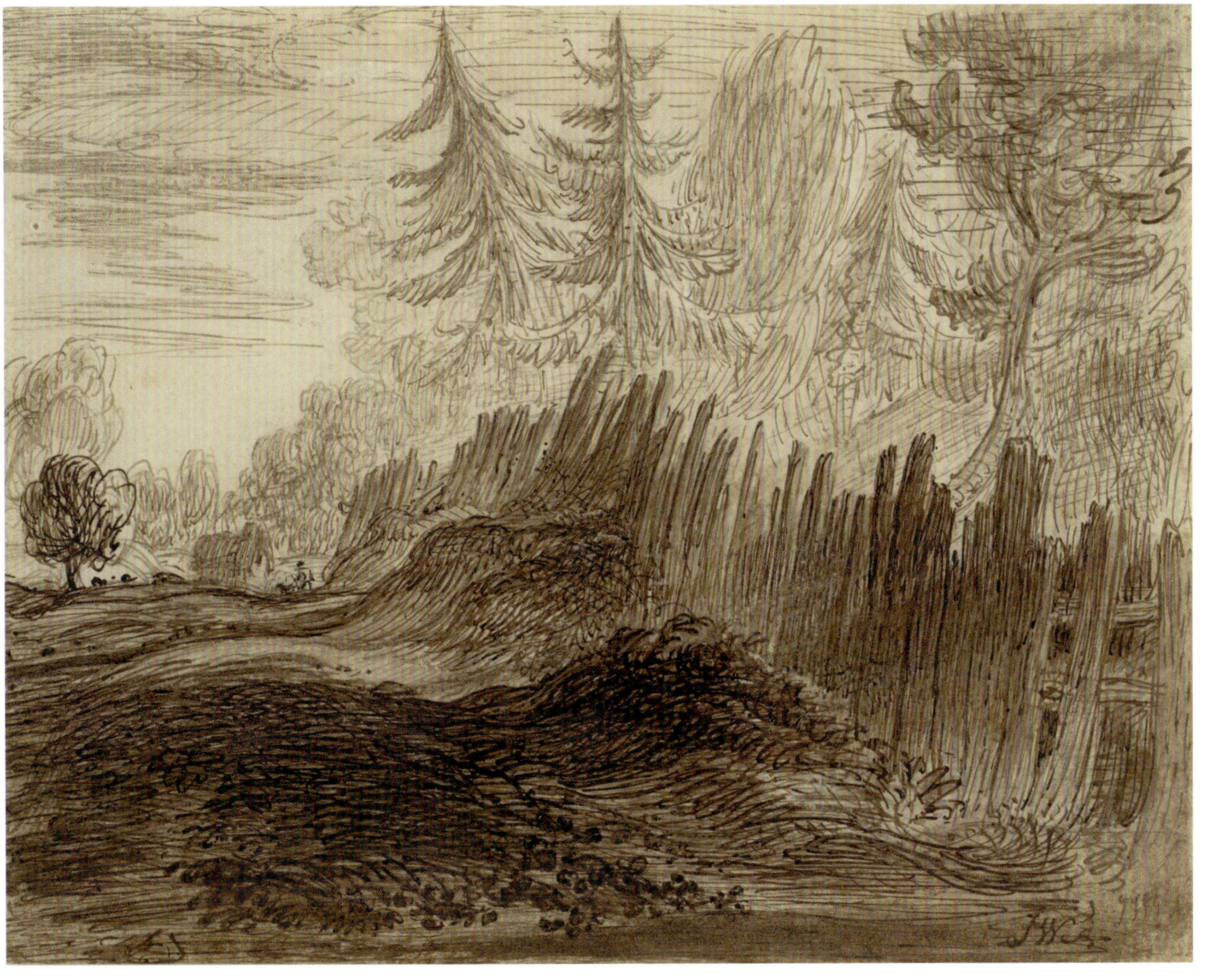

This pen and ink study demonstrates Ward's enduring interest in the work of Flemish seventeenth-century painters, particularly the work of Van Dyck and Rubens.

22 WAITING THE WEATHER

Oil on panel
10½ × 17¾ inches · 267 × 451 mm
Signed *JWD RA* also branded with initials *verso*

LITERATURE: Nygren, 2013, p.366, no.522

EXHIBITED: Possibly, London. Royal Academy, 1846, no.443, as 'Waiting the Weather'; London, Plymouth, Newcastle-upon-Tyne, Leeds & Cardiff, Arts Council exhibition, *James Ward 1769–1859*, 1960, no.47

Ward was an imaginative and inventive landscape painter who captured expansive vistas with same care as the minutiae of individual plants. This present work is a fine example of his interest in light. The luminosity and vivacity of the sky is extraordinarily powerful as Ward shows the light breaking through the clouds in the late afternoon. Nygren proposes that this painting may be *Waiting the Weather* which Ward exhibited at the Royal Academy in 1846. It may also be the work included in the Foster sale (9 May, 1860, lot 32) with the title *Marine View – preparing for bad weather.*

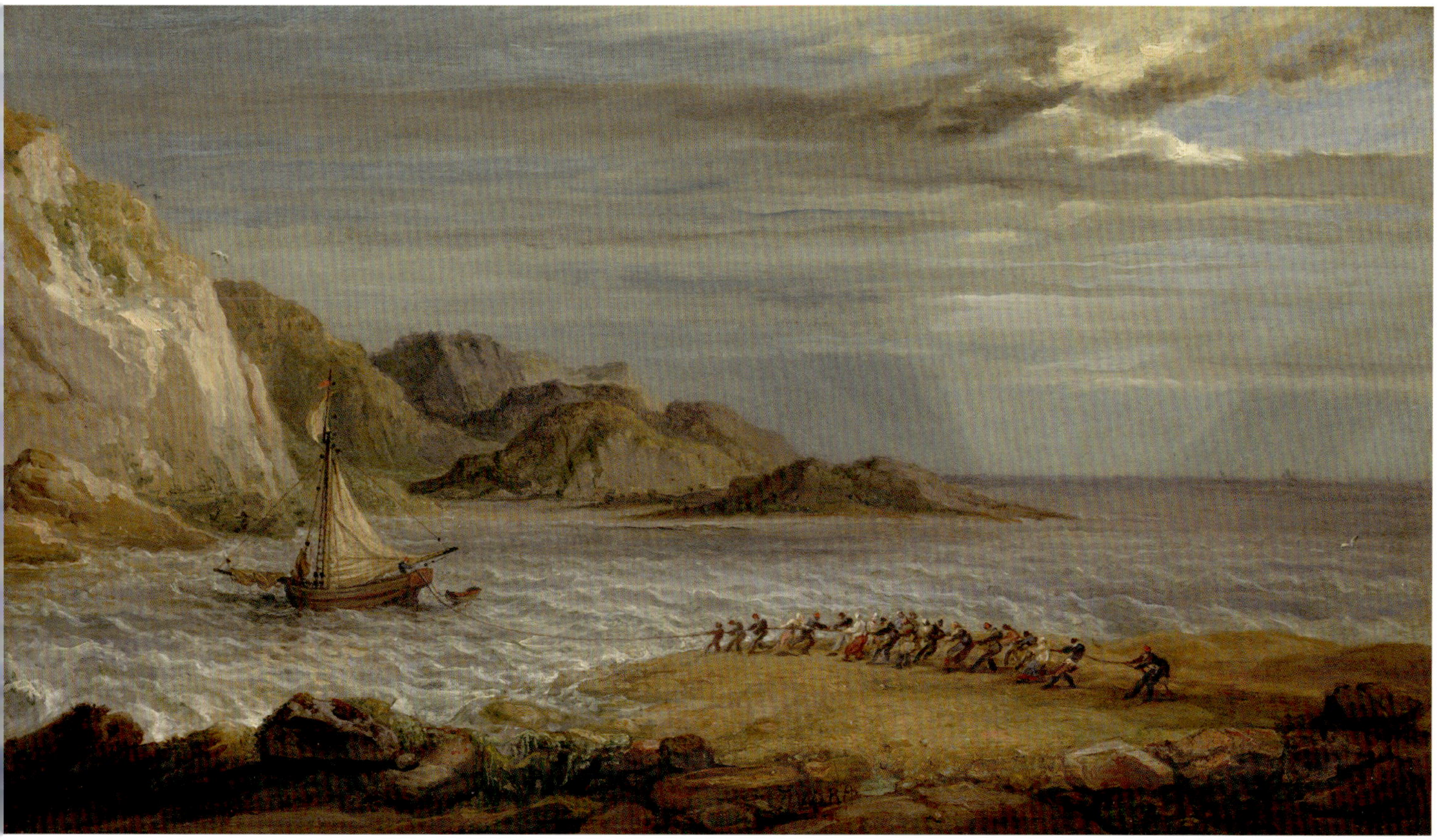

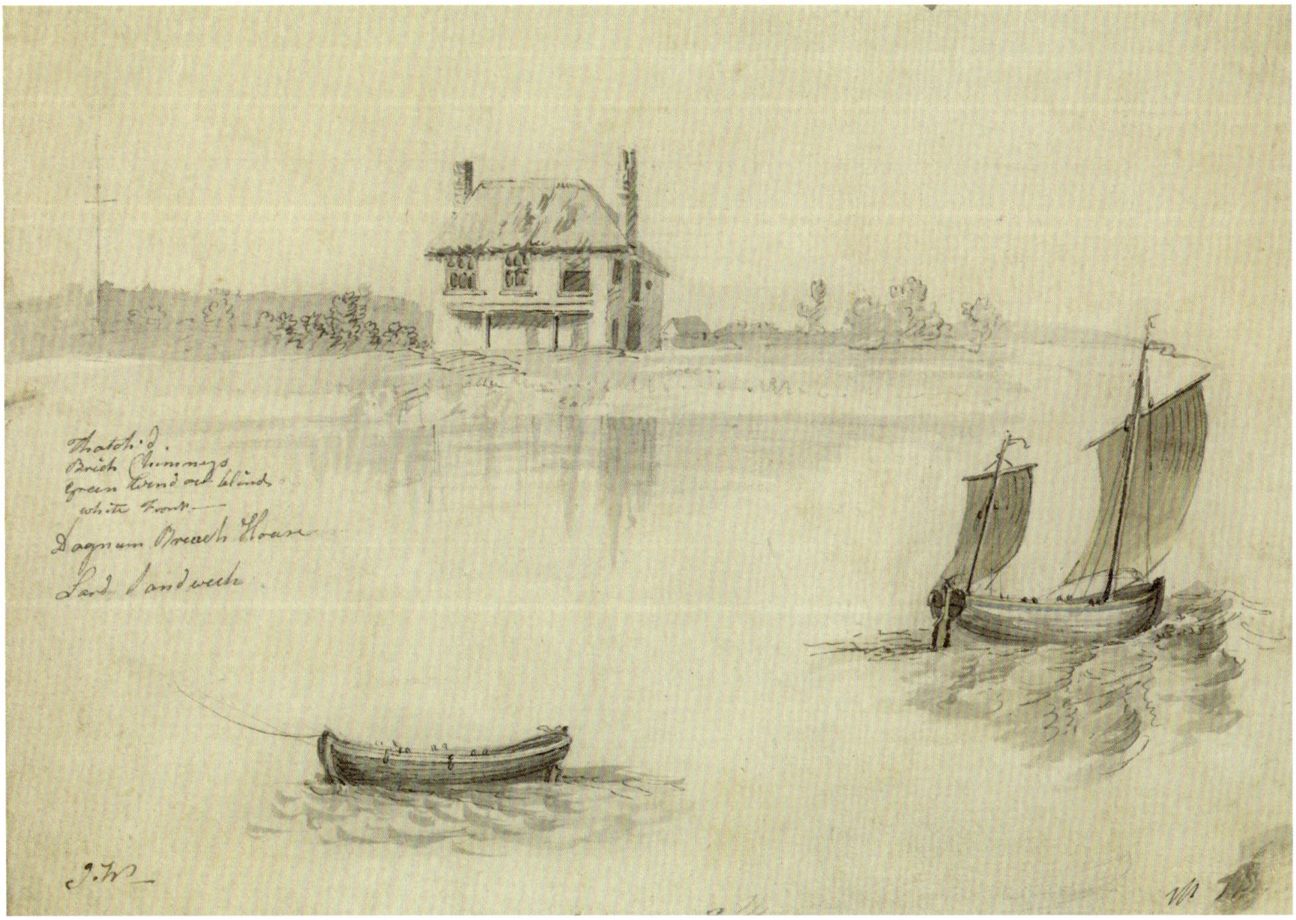
Thatch'd
Brick Chimneys
white Front
Dagnum Breach House
Lord Sandwich
J.W.

23 A FISHING COTTAGE AT DAGENHAM

Pen and ink and coloured wash with grey
6⅛ × 8⅜ inches · 155 × 214 mm
Signed JW and inscribed *Thatch'd / Brick Chimneys / Green window blinds / White front – / Dagnum Breech House / Lord Sandwich*

The drawing possibly depicts what Ward thought was Lord Sandwich's original Breach House but was in fact a fishing cottage built by Richard Webb between 1790 and 1803. Webb sold his interest to Joseph Fry who spent holidays there with his wife Elizabeth Fry, the prison reformer, between 1824 and 1833. The house was demolished in the early 20th century, possibly to make way for the construction of the Ford factory. We are grateful to Mark Watson for identifying the subject of this drawing.

24 A SAILING BARGE

Pencil · 7¼ × 4½ inches · 184 × 115 mm
Signed JWD RA and inscribed in shorthand

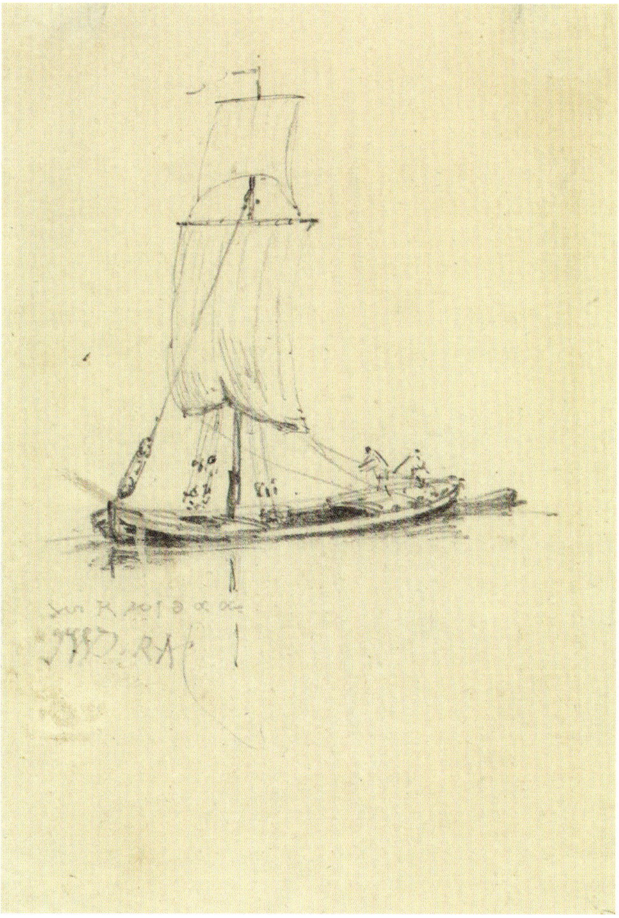

Although a slight study, this rapidly executed but detailed drawing demonstrates Ward's method of sketching *en plein air*. In his desire to capture the scene before him, his pencil strokes have been reduced to staccato lines and dots and dashes, which combine to create an energised study.

25 A CHURCH AND WINDMILLS ON THE BANKS OF AN ESTUARY

Pencil · 2½ × 4⅛ inches · 63 × 104 mm
Signed: *JWD*

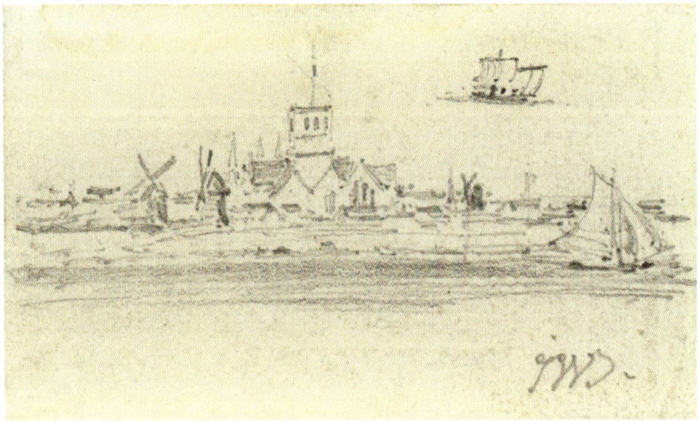

The present landscape is characteristic of the fleeting studies Ward made whilst on his frequent sketching tours of Britain. The finely observed view of a town clearly shows the influence of Dutch seventeenth-century landscape painting on Ward's work, a fact emphasised by the prominent windmills and sailing boat.

26 FIGURES WAITING BY BEACHED BOATS ON A ROCKY COASTLINE

Oil on panel
7 × 11⅜ inches · 180 × 288 mm
Signed with *IWRA* brand on *verso*

COLLECTIONS: Oglander, Nunwell, Isle of Wight

This characteristic oil study of circa 1810 is reminiscent of the subject-matter beloved by Ward's brother-in-law, George Morland. Ward produced a number of similar compositions depicting coastal scenes presumably prompted, in part, by Morland's success. In 1810 he completed a painting of a *Coastal Scene in Storm* for the great patron and collector Sir John Leicester which he exhibited at the British Institution in 1810 (294) a sketch for which is in the collection of Nottingham Castle Museum and Art Gallery. Like the present composition, the Nottingham sketch concentrates on the shoreline and figures rather than the seascape. Although evidently fascinated by the old fishermen and their environment he was apparently not a good sailor; amongst his notes from a trip to Margate in October 1819 he records being 'dreadfully & dangerously sick' after a rough boat trip (Nygren, 2013, p.45).

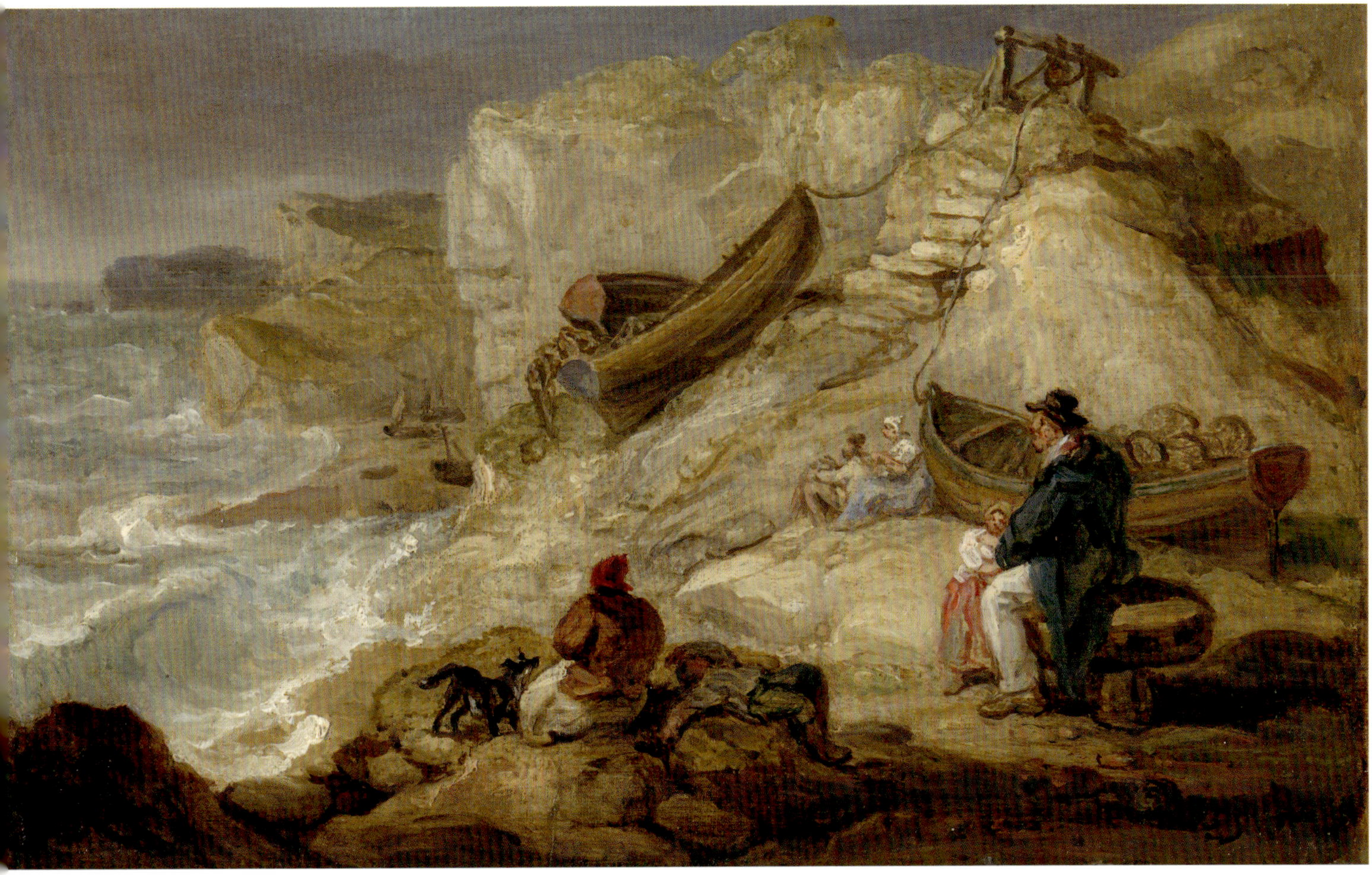

27 CADER IDRIS ON A CLOUDY DAY

Pen and ink and wash £3,200
3⅜ × 6½ inches · 86 × 165 mm
Signed: *JWD RA*

My Cader Idris in cloud
2009 Andrew Wyld £2,000 (I pd. £1,750)

This spirited study is closely related to two similarly handled studies views taken from the summit of Cader Idris (formerly Summerhayes collection) which were made in 1807 when Ward ascended the mountain in search of Ellis Thomas, the brother of the 'Starving Woman' Mary Thomas.

28 MOONLIT LANDSCAPE

Pen and ink and wash
3⅜ × 4¾ inches · 86 × 121 mm
Signed: *JW*

There is another drawing of the same terrace and view, but in daylight, in a private collection. It may be of one of the properties of Ward's patron, the Earl of Powis, perhaps Oakley Park, Bromfield, Shropshire. It could have been made on one of his visits with Powis, one having taken place in 1817.

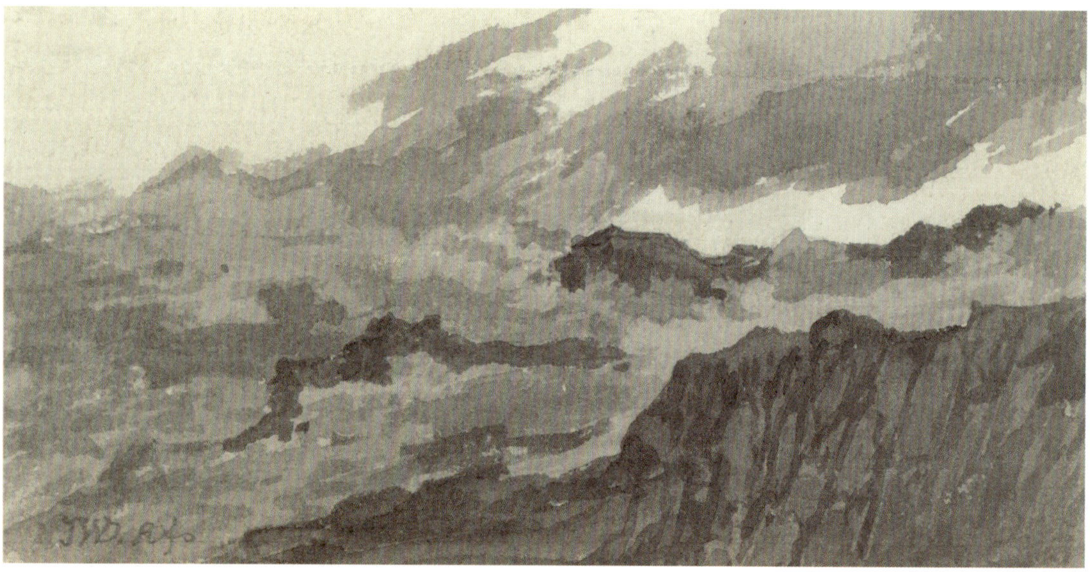

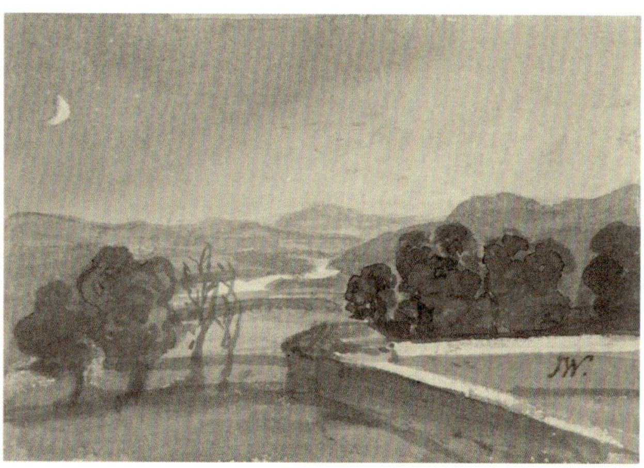

29 MR RICH'S COTTAGE, ST ALBANS

Pen and ink and wash
9 × 9½ inches · 229 × 241 mm
Signed *JWD* and inscribed: *Mr Rich's cottage nr St Albans*

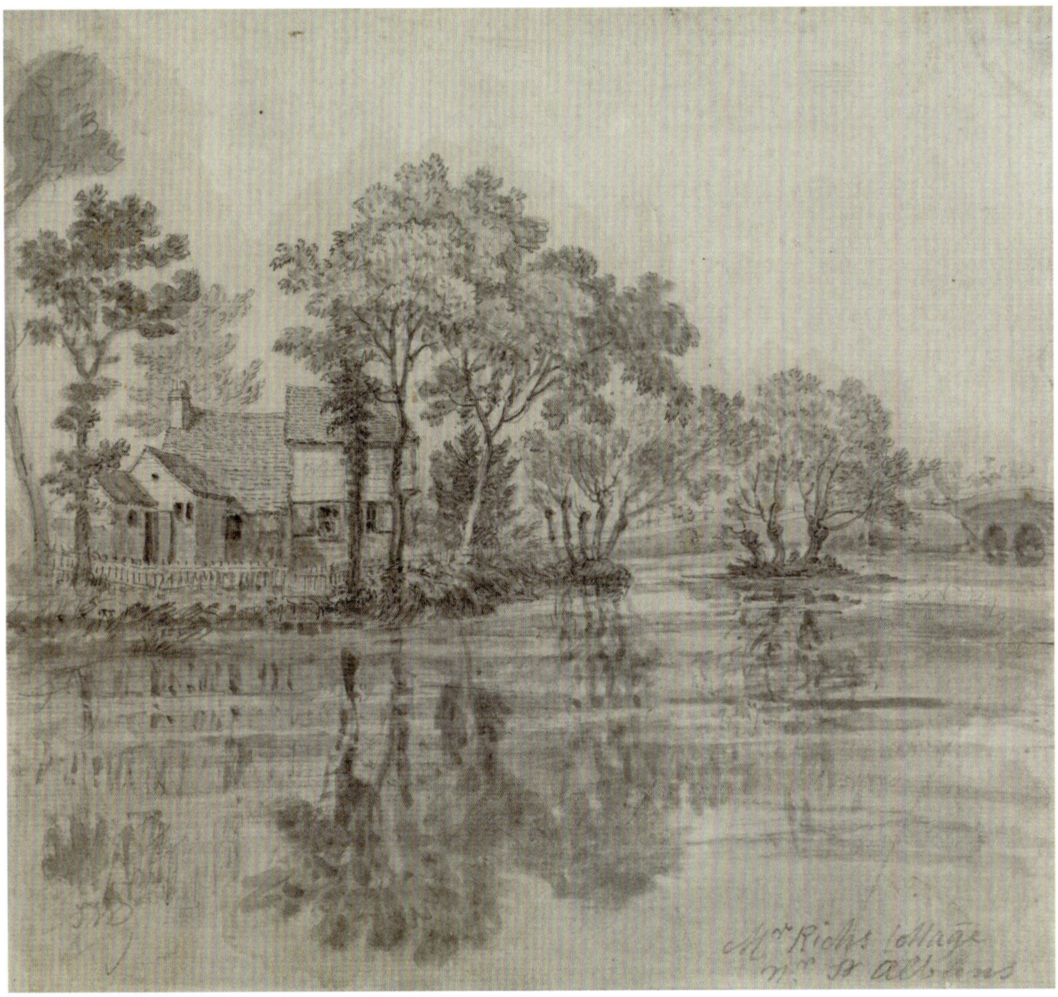

This cottage may possibly have belonged to the Mr Rich and his wife who Ward knew in London and who took care of Ward's wife Mary. Ward's two sons, James Claude and Somerville, were both at school in St Albans in 1820–21. It is likely this work was completed during one of his visits.

30 AN INDUSTRIAL LANDSCAPE: A SMELTING WORKS

Oil on panel
6 × 3¾ inches · 152 × 95 mm
Signed with brand *IWRA* verso

LITERATURE: Nygren, 1976, p.245, repr. fig. 268

Ward lived through a period of rapid industrialisation; however, like many of his contemporaries he rarely depicted industrial scenes. Instead Ward preferred picturesque rural buildings which he frequently depicted as almost organic aspects of the landscape although as Nygren has pointed out (*op.cit.*) the present work can be seen as being related to a small group of paintings in which man's selfishness is represented by fire. It is this romantic spirit which infuses the current picture. Although Ward would have been familiar with the major copper smelting areas around Swansea and the iron smelting works in Shropshire he chose not to show the grim reality of these industrial processes. Ward instead chose to depict the works' chimneys silhouetted against the blaze, making them appear like the ruins of a medieval abbey or castle. By depicting the process at night, Ward continues a tradition of showing industrial processes in a nocturnal setting begun by Joseph Wright of Derby and Philip de Loutherbourg in the previous generation following in the eighteenth century interest in the 'Sublime'. Amongst Ward's other industrial subjects are *Coal works, the property of Ralph Lambton Esq, as seen from a window in Barton House, Durham*, exhibited at the Royal Academy in 1845 (no.218) and *Iron Works near Swa*nsea which he showed at the British Institution in 1846 (no.340).

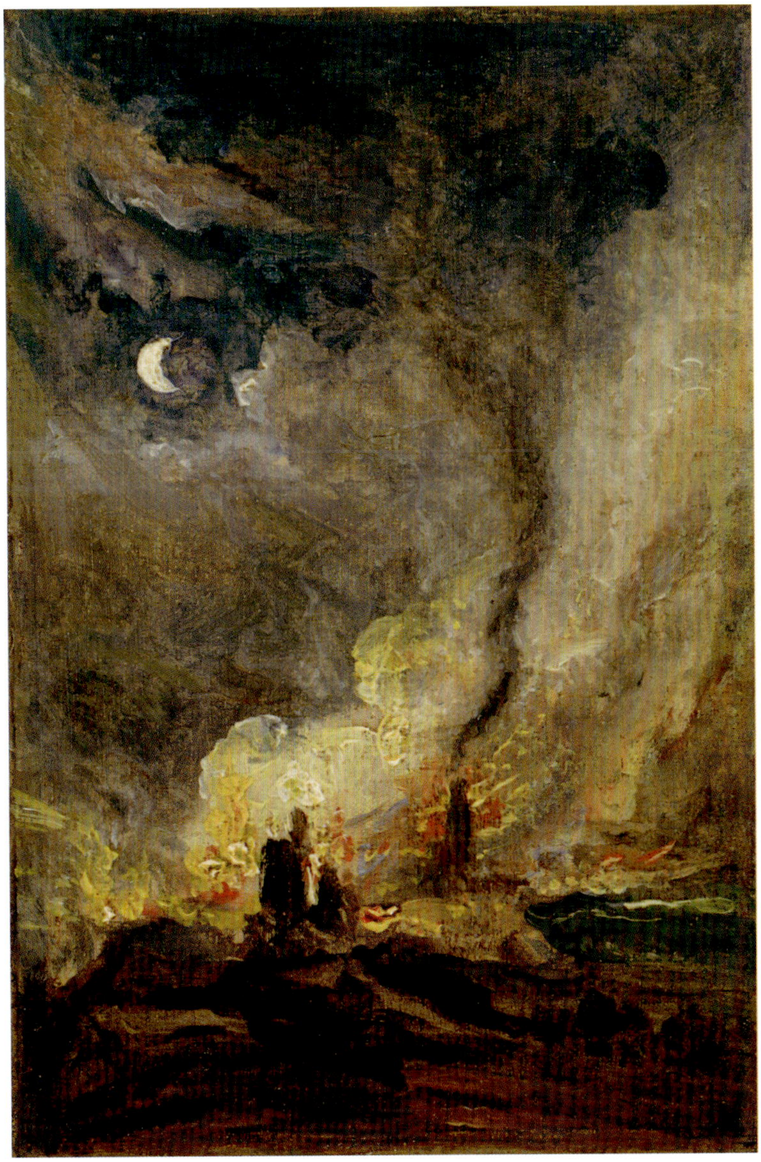

31 A ROCKY STREAM £950

Pencil and black chalk
9⅜ × 10½ inches · 240 × 266 mm
Signed *JWD RA* and inscribed with artist's shorthand

The present sheet is characteristic of the kind of bold fluid sketches Ward made on his frequent tours around Britain. Covered in Ward's distinctive shorthand the sheet would most likely have been intended for use in his studio.

32 A PAGE FROM A SKETCHBOOK WITH STUDIES OF TREES, PLANTS, FIGURES AND A STAG

Pencil · 9⅜ × 14¾ inches · 240 × 376 mm

Ward has minutely observed the trunk of a tree with its bare branches and combines that scrupulously observed study with a pair of figures conversing and a running stag. Our drawing is close in technique to a smaller drawing of a fallen branch of *c.*1800–05 in the G.J. Ward collection.

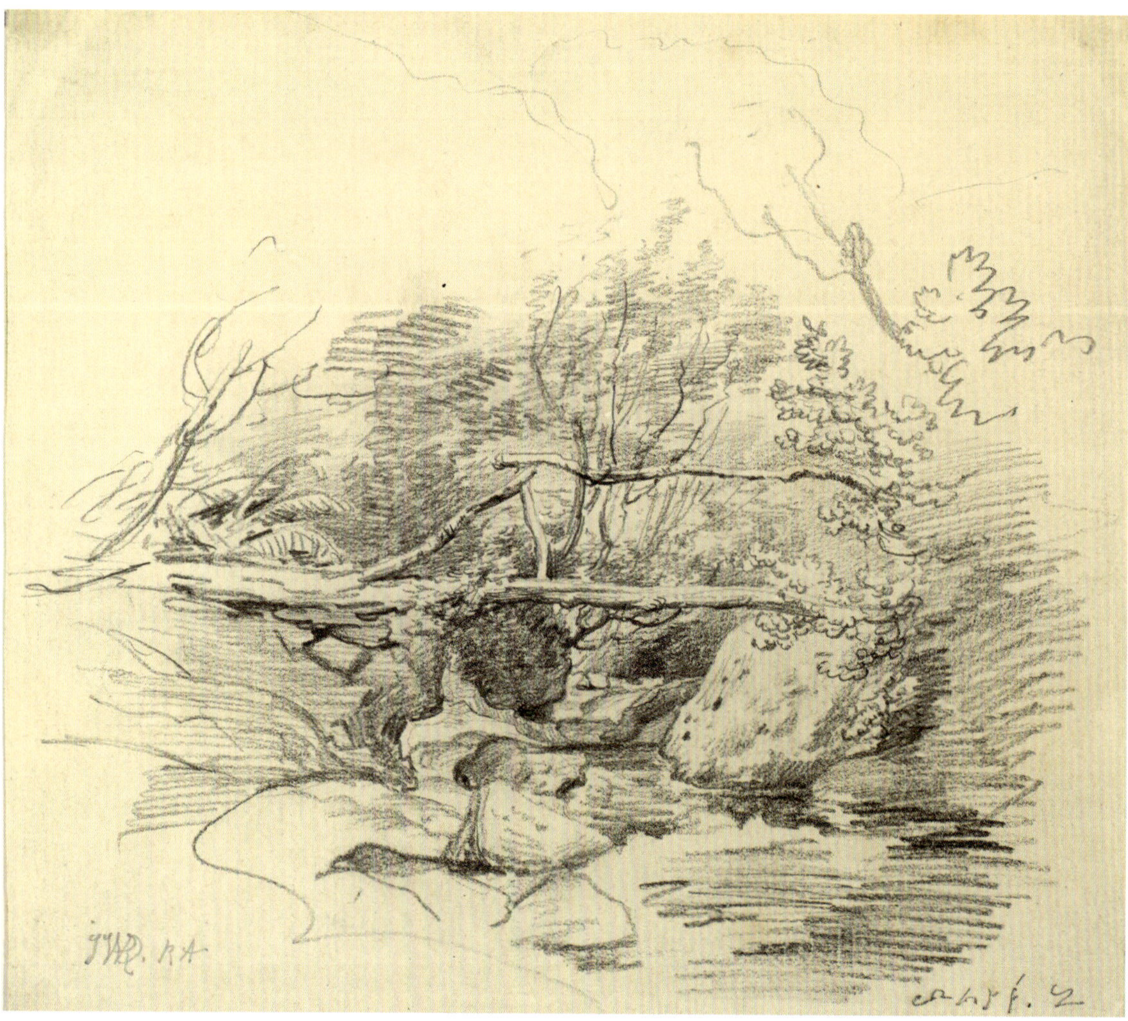

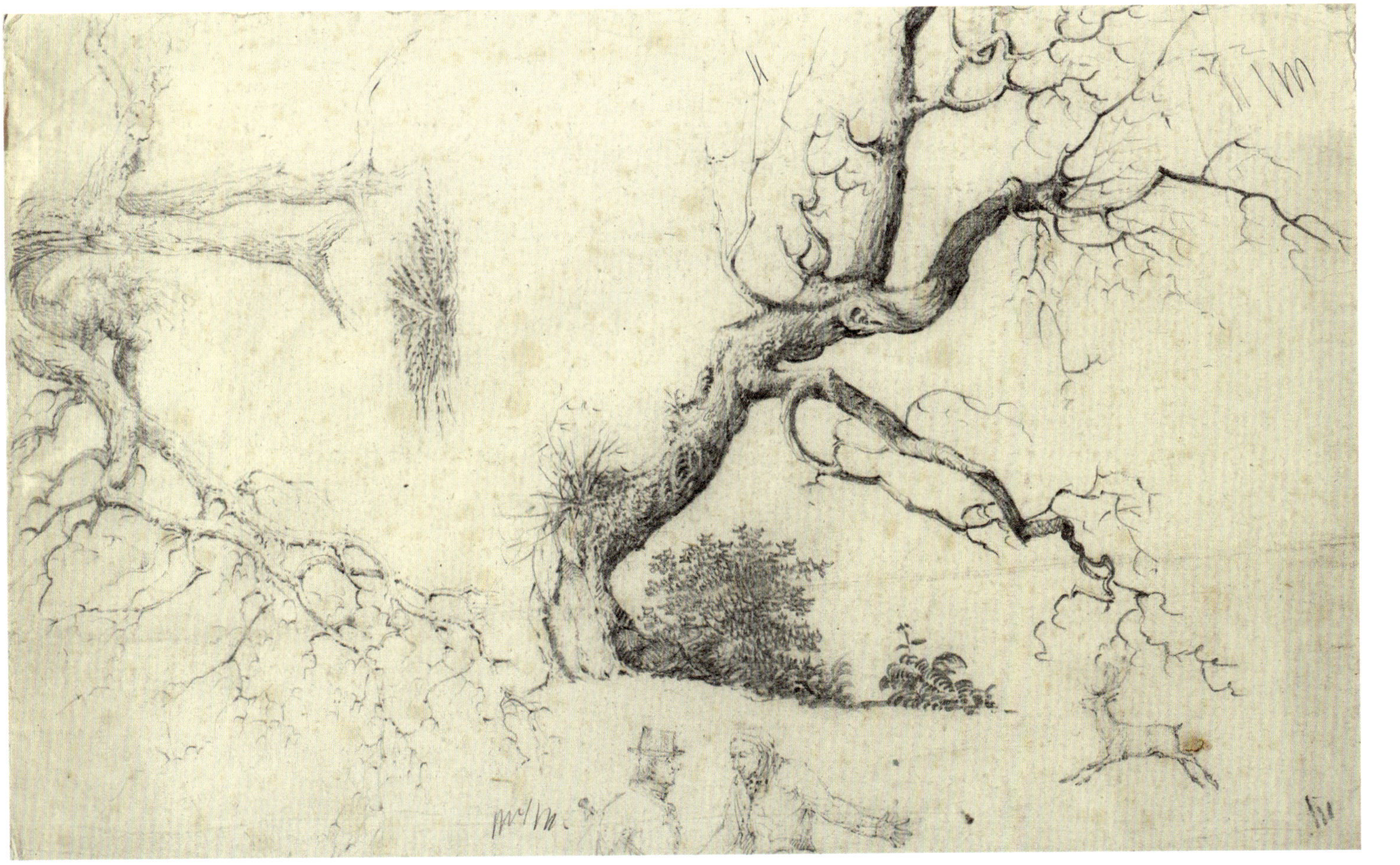

33 A TREE TRUNK

Watercolour and Pencil · 7⅝ × 8½ inches · 194 × 215 mm
Signed: *JWD*

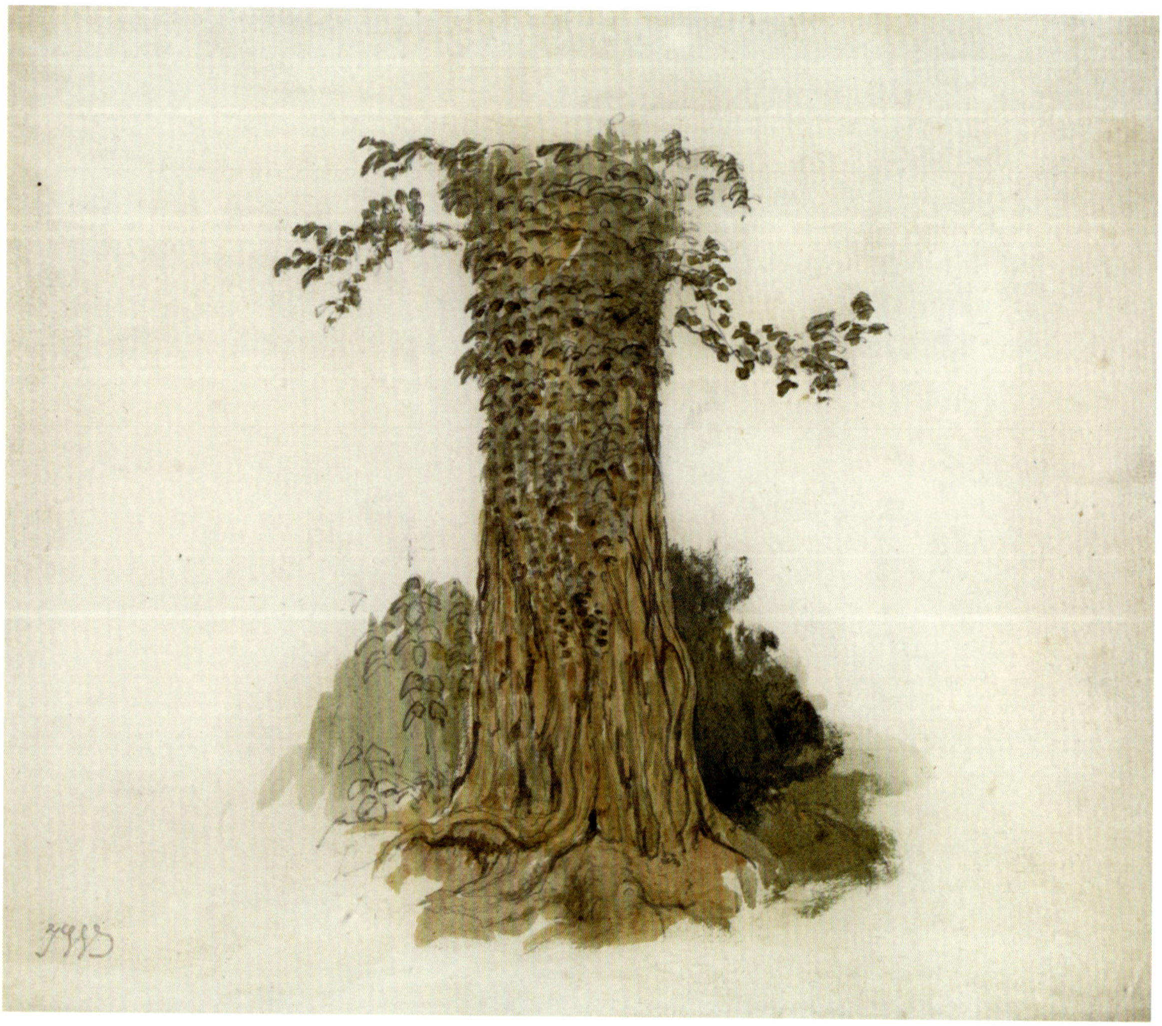

This is a rare example of Ward working primarily in watercolour when producing a *plein air* study. He occasionally explored landscape in wash but rarely in colour. The majority of Ward's rapid sketches appear to have been executed in pencil, often with colour notes and shorthand annotations as a reference with which to work from when back in the studio.

34 WATERLILIES

Watercolour over Pencil · 4⅝ × 6⅞ inches · 118 × 176 mm
Signed: *JWD RA*

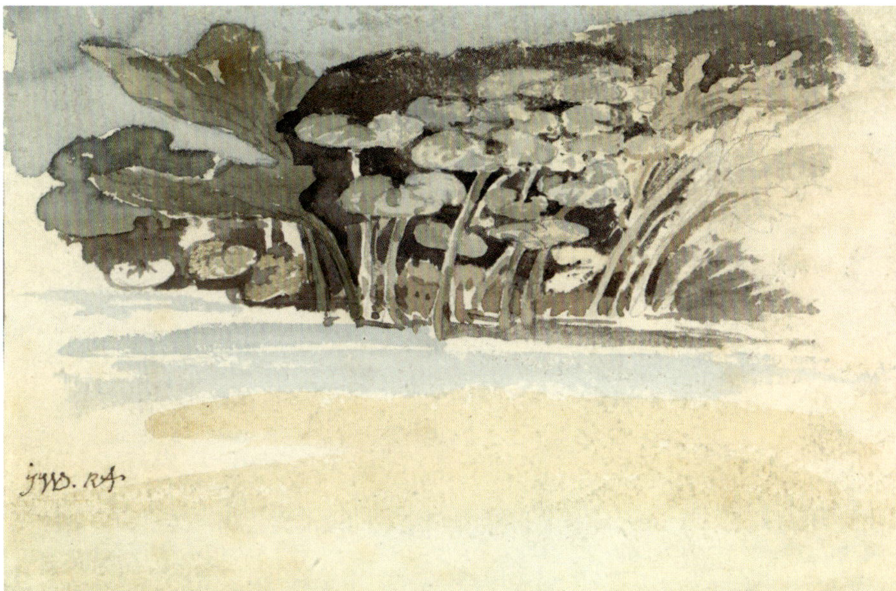

As in the case of the study of a tree trunk this watercolour is an unusual example of Ward working in watercolour when sketching outdoors. The present study demonstrates his sensitivity and skill at rendering forms with wash.

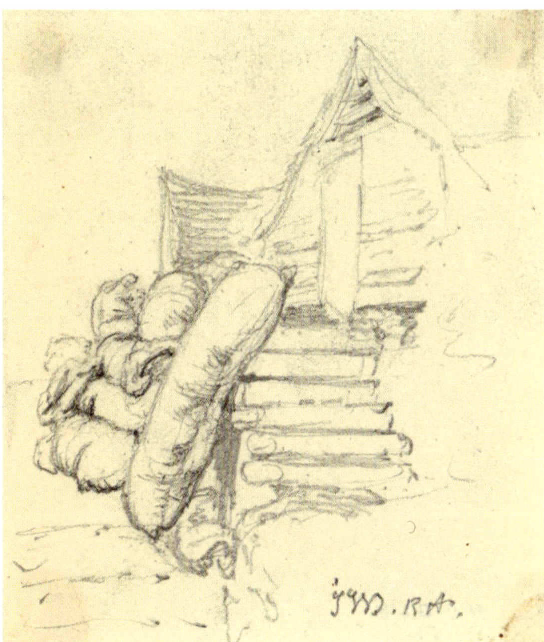

35 WOOL SACKS STACKED BY THE STEPS TO A STORE

Pencil · 4½ × 3¾ inches · 114 × 95 mm
Signed: *JWD RA*

This pencil study shows bales of wool stacked against the side of a house. This type of sketch is characteristic of Ward's interest in the routine scenes of agricultural life and his deep engagement with rural life in Britain.

II
Figure Studies

Although Ward did not attend the Royal Academy schools, where life drawing was part of the young artist's training, he did attend lectures held by Joshua Brookes, where both human and animal anatomy was studied. Brookes' classes had the additional benefits of being significantly cheaper and smaller than those held at the Royal Academy and students were also allowed to dissect and draw corpses for a small additional fee. Ward's understanding of both human and animal form is amply demonstrated in the competence shown in even the most rapidly executed of his sketches included in this catalogue.

Like many of his contemporaries, Ward was fascinated with the study of physiognomy and he produced numerous drawings which explored this concept, it was undoubtedly this which prompted Ward to make the sensitive portrait of the murderer Joseph Wittingham (cat.49). The most striking is the oil study of a man's head clearly registering fear or terror (cat.42). Ward's curiosity meant that he frequently made studies of the unusual or exotic figures who came to London, such as the Cossacks in the suite of Tsar Alexander I who arrived in 1814 (cat.46). However the largest body of studies is the sensitive, fleeting sketches he made of figures encountered on his travels around Britain. Frequently depictions of rural labourers, they demonstrate Ward's remarkable powers of observation.

36 THE ANGEL OF BETHESDA

Oil on canvas · 13¼ × 21¼ inches · 338 × 540 mm
Painted *circa* 1816–17

COLLECTIONS: Mary Ann Garle, a gift from the artist; Thomas Garle; Garle sale, Christie's, 24 May 1862 (31), purchased by Capp; John Allnutt; Allnutt sale, Christie's, 19 June 1863 (217), purchased by Cook; Desmond FitzGerald, The Knight of Glin

EXHIBITED: By the artist, 1822 at his Newman Street studio and exhibition rooms, no.101, as *The Angel of Bethesda*

This is a *modello* for a large (96 × 128 inches) painting which was commissioned by John Knight of Lea Castle, Worcestershire in 1816 and exhibited at the British Institution in 1818 as *The Pool of Bethesda*. The painting, which cost £200 has been lost.

Ward, keen to prove that he was more than a 'mere' animal painter produced mythological, allegorical, religious and historical paintings throughout his career. It is interesting that almost all of these, including the finished painting of this subject, received mixed reviews. The reviewer in *The Literary Gazette* following its exhibition felt that it: '*brings … some of the finest efforts of ancient art, and has a love of colour, and texture of execution extremely difficult to attain.* However, they continue, b*ut these belong only to the lower qualities of such a subject. Some of the figures are unnatural abortions, and the angel a hard and pedantic form, which not only "troubles the waters" but annoys every feeling of good art*.' (*The London Literary Gazette and Journal of belle lettres, arts, sciences, etc.*, 1818, p.105). Knight however must have been happy with the picture, not only did he pay for it, but he continued to support Ward and to commission work from him.

The present work being smaller in scale than the finished picture, probably avoids the issues that Ward would have faced when working on the scale of the finished work.

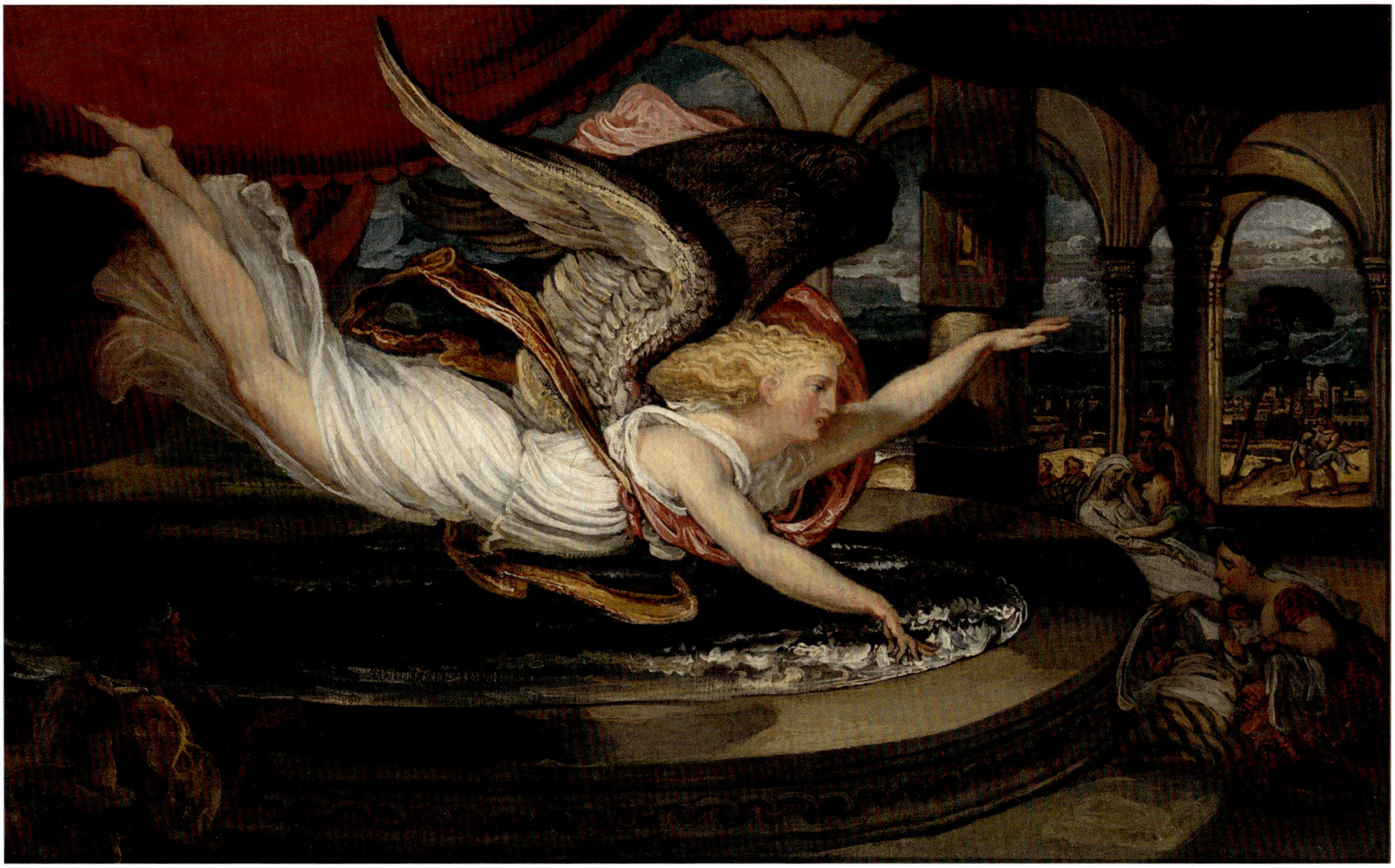

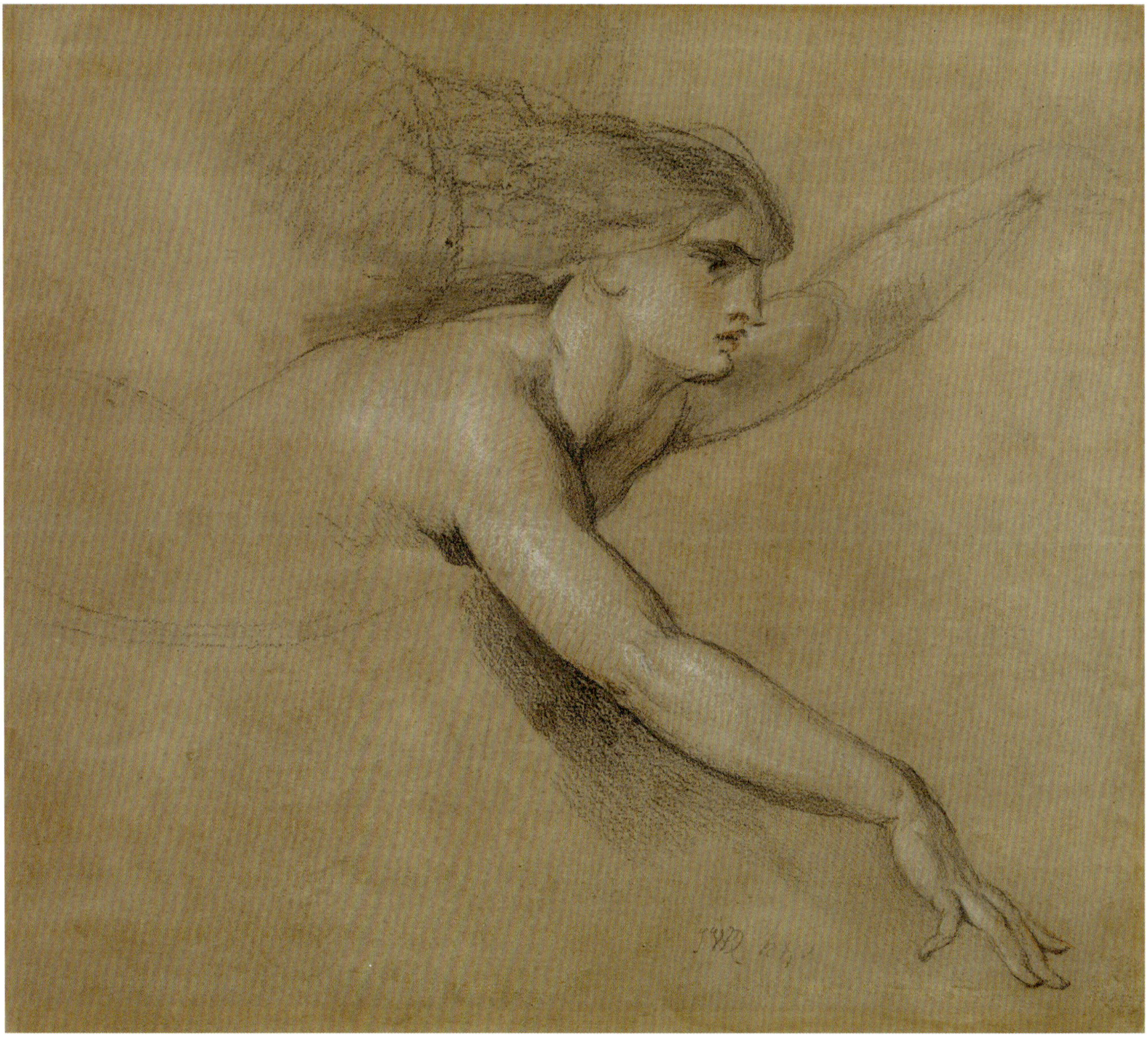

37 STUDY OF AN ANGEL FOR 'THE POOL OF BETHESDA'

Coloured chalks on buff paper
12½ × 13½ inches · 311 × 345 mm
Signed *JWD RA*

The present sketch is a study for the figure of the angel in Ward's painting, *The Pool of Bethesda*, which has survived in the *modello* (cat.36). This is a rare example of an 'academic' study for a finished painting; in the manner of life drawings of the period, it is executed in black chalk with white heightening. The work perhaps underlines Ward's ambitions to become a history painter. In Ward's diary entry for Thursday 10th April 1818 he noted that he had: 'given the angel to Mrs Garle'; a reference to Mary Ann, the wife of Thomas Garle, one of Ward's major patrons. Nygren, who had earlier proposed that this drawing was the work given to Mrs Garle, indicates that the oil study or *modello* may have been the gift. It is interesting to note that whilst the overall composition has remained the same from this study to the painting, the angel's expression has softened and her features become more feminine.

38 A SEATED FEMALE NUDE

Pencil and watercolour on laid paper
7¼ × 4⅝ inches · 183 × 119 mm
Signed: *JW*

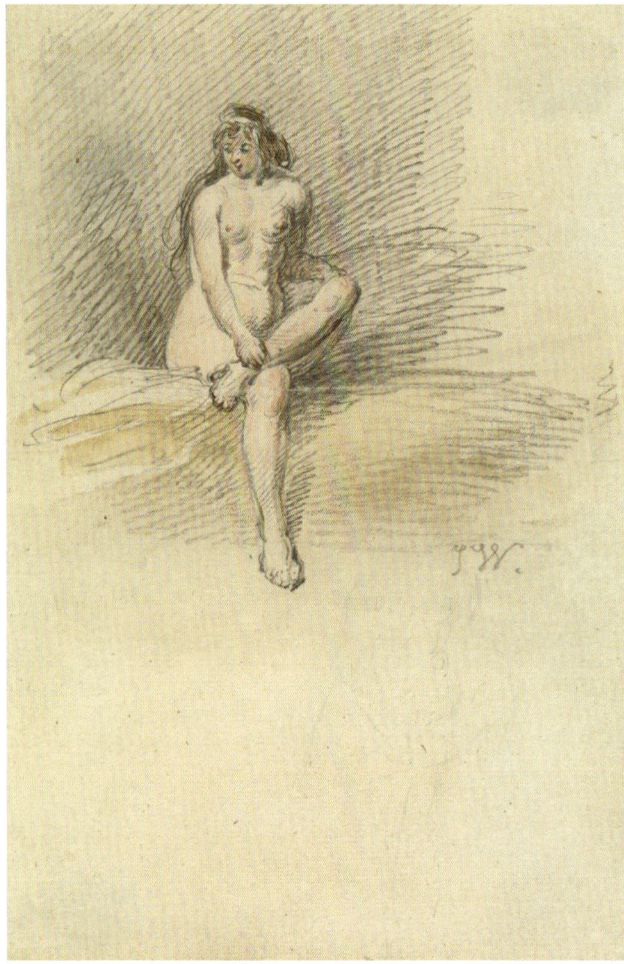

39 LIFE STUDY OF A FEMALE MODEL

Pencil · 4 × 5 inches · 102 × 127 mm
Signed: *JWD*

The present drawing appears to be a rare study of a female nude drawn from life. Another study is recorded of the same sitter from a slightly different view point.

40 STUDIES FOR 'VENUS RISING FROM HER COUCH'

Pencil · 6½ × 7⅞ inches · 165 × 200 mm
Signed: *JWD RA*

This group of sketches are compositional sketches relating to Ward's 1828 painting, *Venus Rising from her Couch*, exhibited at the Royal Academy in 1830 [no.135] and now in the Yale Center for British Art. Ward continued to paint grand subject pictures throughout his life and in 1830 – apart from *Venus Rising from her Couch* – he also exhibited *The Fall of Phaeton* as well as *Diana at her bath, disturbed by Actaeon* at the Royal Academy; the composition shown on the lower left of our sheet appears to be an early idea for that composition. Ward did not gain favourable criticism for his efforts. *Venus Rising from her Couch* was described in *The Gentleman's Magazine* as possessing: 'not one redeeming virtue to atone for its indelicacy' (*The Gentleman's Magazine*, May 1830, p.445). Whilst the *London Literary gazette* enlarged on this criticism when it stated: 'badly drawn, badly coloured and what is much worse indelicate' (*The London Literary Gazette and Journal of belle lettres, arts, sciences, etc.*, 1830, p.323). The present preliminary study shows Ward working out the composition as well as his attempts to produce a bold nude study, in the manner of the Renaissance models by Titian he so much admired. The closeness of the final painting to the drawing boldly framed with a thick black line underlines the importance of such studies in Ward's creative process.

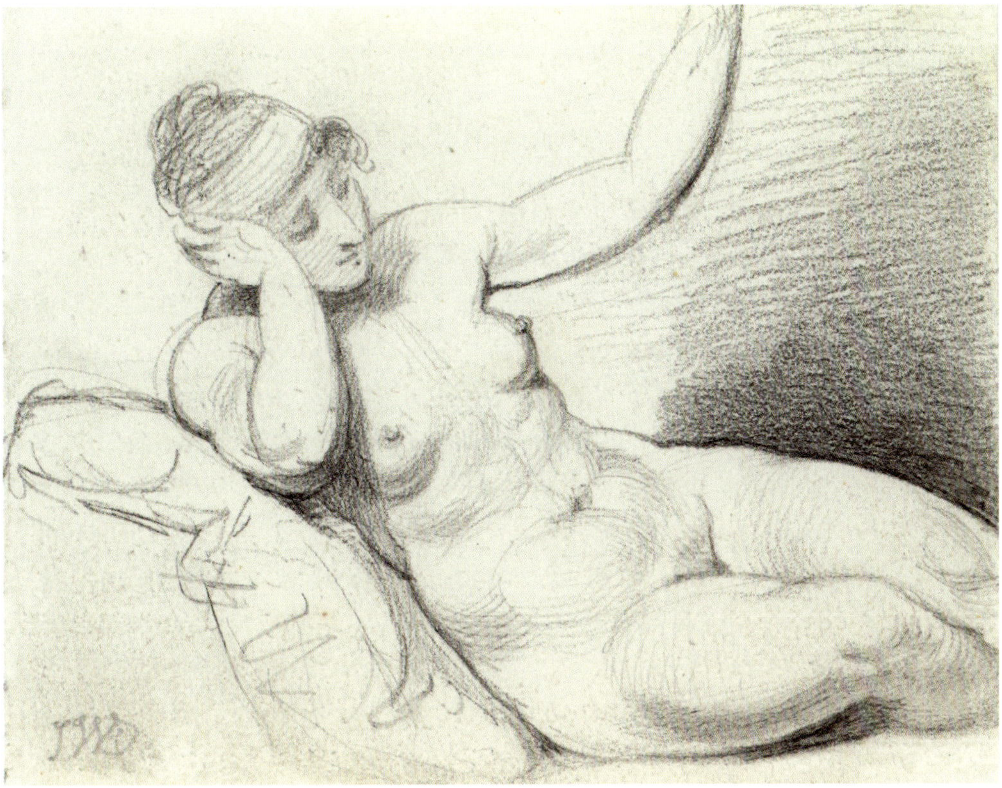
TWD

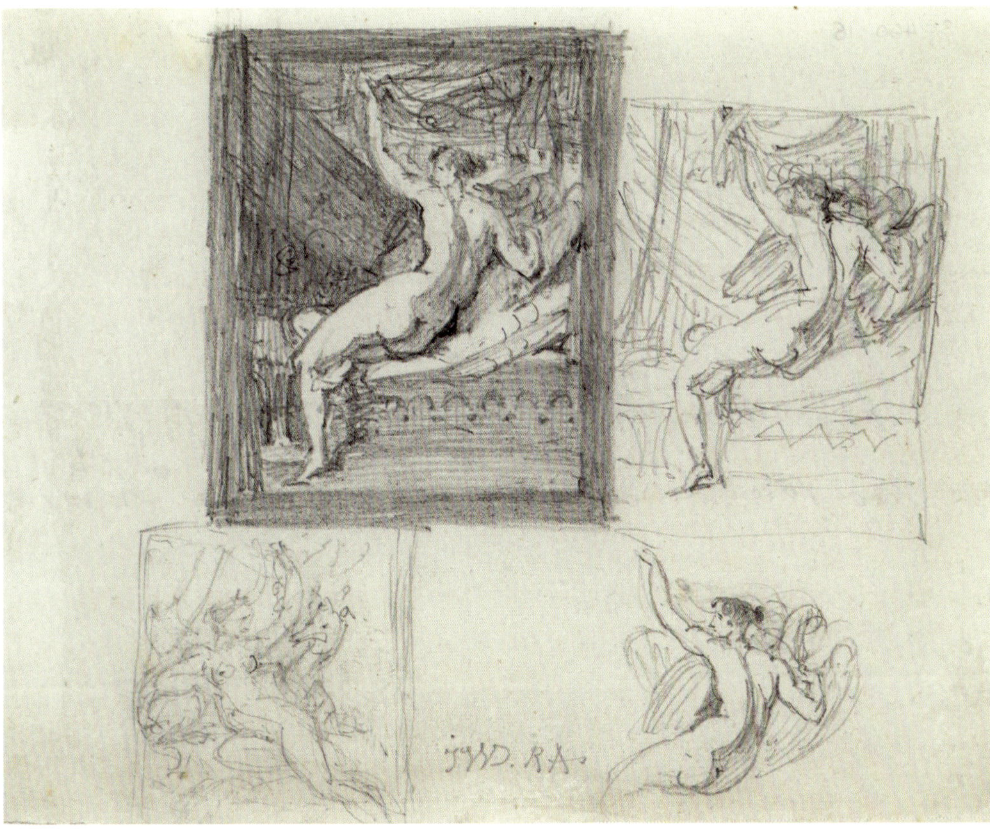
TWD. RA.

41 A PROFILE OF A BEARDED FIGURE

Pen and ink · 10¼ × 7¼ inches · 259 × 183 mm
Signed: *JW RA*
With sketch of a face and with pen marks *verso*

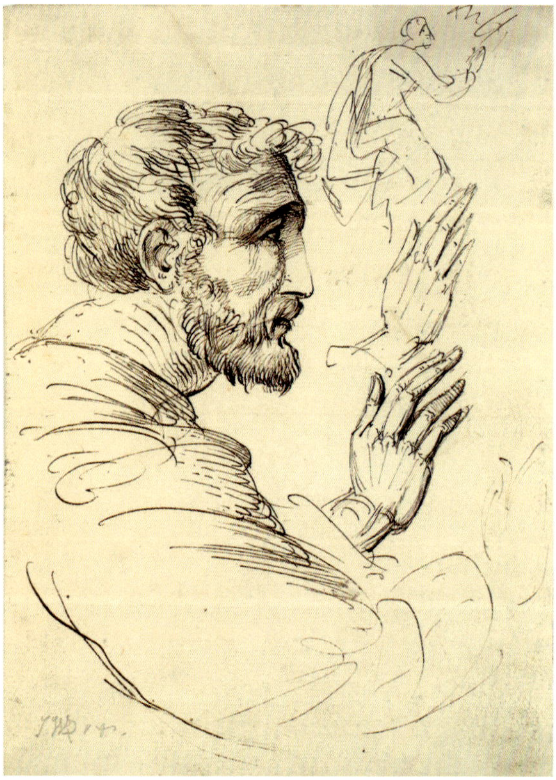

This profile pen and ink study recalls figures of the Apostles from Raphael's tapestry cartoons, although it does not seem to be a direct copy. A similarly treated drawing of three classical figures of *c.*1811 was formerly in the Summerhayes collection. The tapestry cartoons were accessible to artists at the beginning of the nineteenth century as they were leant to the British Institution and Royal Academy by the Prince Regent. Ward records copying a head from *The Death of Ananias* in March 1818 at the Academy (Nygren, 2013, p.33). Ward also spent much time and effort making careful transcriptions of the Elgin marbles. Copies and studies such as this can be seen as part of Ward's efforts to become an historical painter.

42 'DESPAIR' – A HEAD EXPRESSING TERROR OR FEAR: A STUDY FOR 'THE WATERLOO ALLEGORY'

Oil on canvas · 17¾ × 12¾ inches · 451 × 324 mm
Signed *JW RA*, also branded verso *IWRA*

LITERATURE: Nygren, 1976, p.134, repr. fig. 175

This is almost certainly the painting exhibited by Ward at Newman Street in 1822 (no.17) as *Despair*; and it may also be the work subsequently shown at Newman Street in 1841 (no.96) as *A Study from an Italian Sailor* which Ward identifies in the text as a study for *The Waterloo Allegory*. The treatment of emotion is almost certainly based on Charles Le Brun's representation of terror or fright in *Heads: Representing the Various Passions of the Soul* which would probably have been known to Ward from an edition published in London in 1813. At least one drawing survived by Ward in which he directly copied the engraving of one of Le Brun's heads.

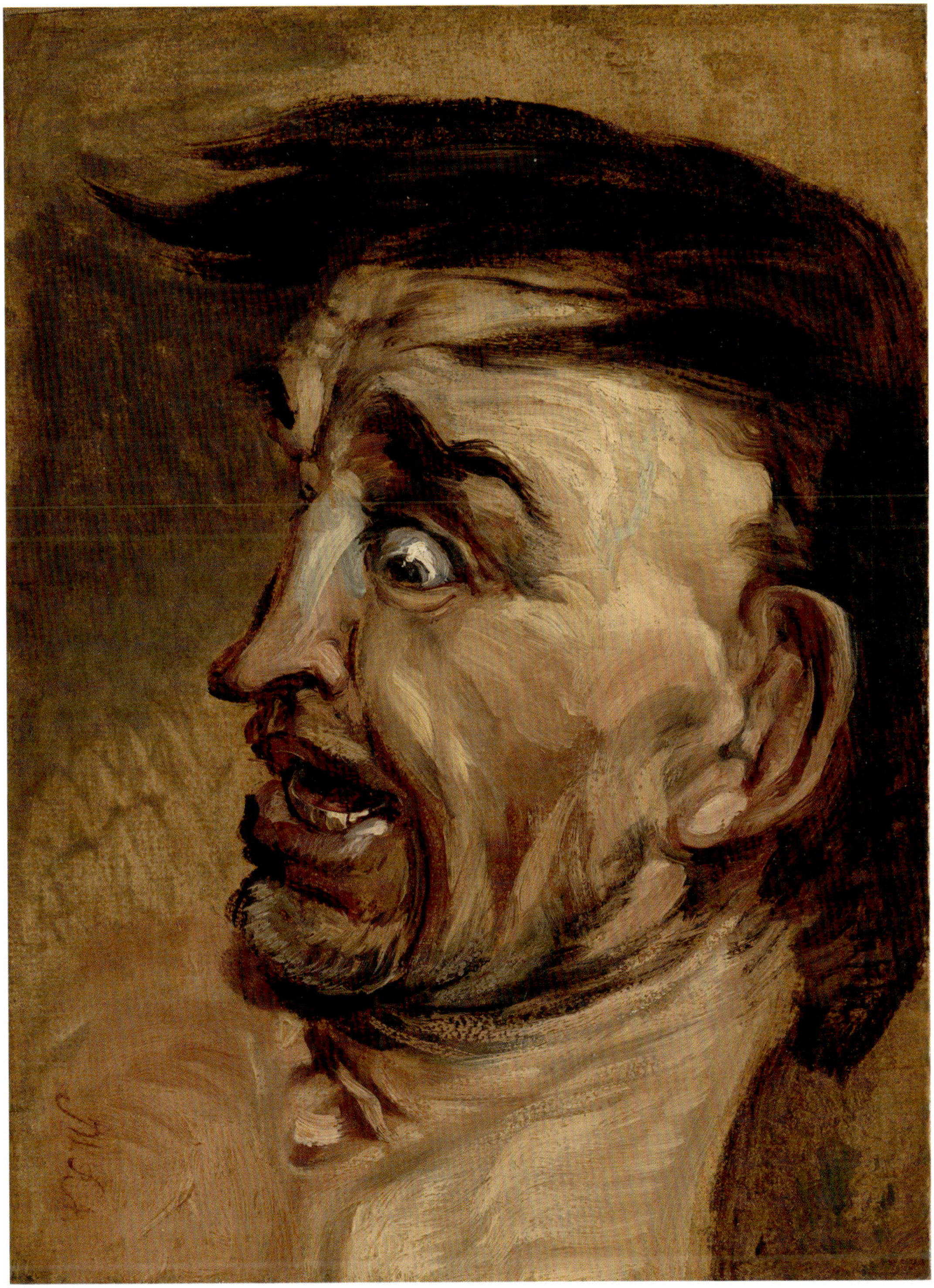

43 THESEUS AND THE CRETAN BULL

Pencil · 10¾ × 14⅞ inches · 273 × 378 mm
Signed: *JWD RA*

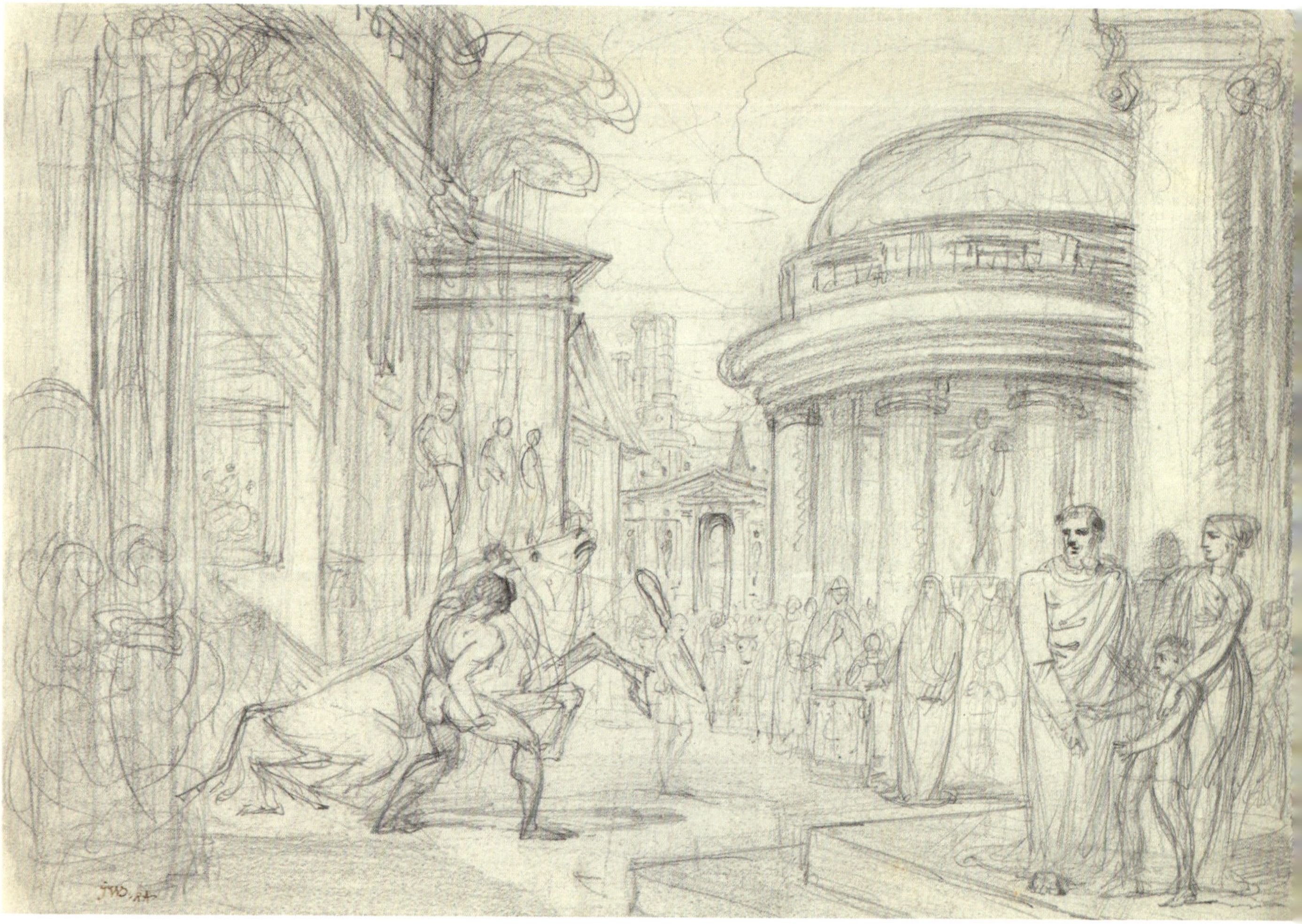

Ward was clearly interested in classical mythology; throughout his career, he produced various paintings exploring classical subjects. Ward made a number of drawings of the Elgin Marbles at the British Museum in 1817. The present sheet is a fully developed study for depicting Theseus wrestling with the Cretan bull. The story depicts the legendary bull of Crete being subdued by Theseus, before being taken to Athens and sacrificed.

Ward's fascination with bulls undoubtedly attracted him to the story although this and the related drawing (cat.44) seem to be his only handlings of the subject and he never produced a full-scale painting depicting the scene.

44 THESEUS AND THE CRETAN BULL

Pen and ink · 7¼ × 9 inches · 184 × 228 mm
Signed: *JWD RA*

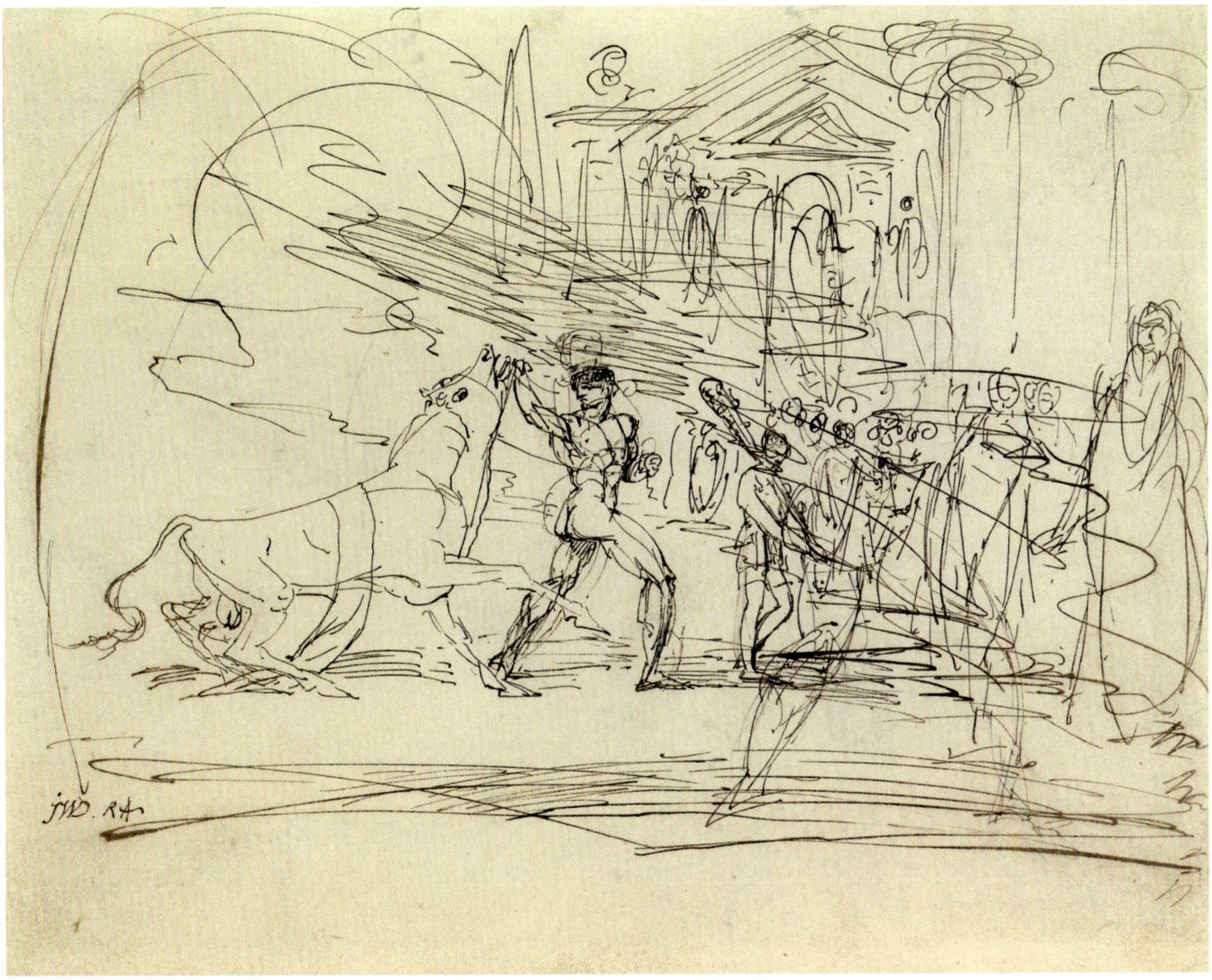

A spirited pen and ink study for the composition he developed more fully in our related drawing (cat.43) Despite Ward's evident fascination with the subject – a bull of legendary strength pitted against a man – he never developed the composition into a full-scale oil painting.

45 STUDY FOR AN EQUESTRIAN PORTRAIT

Pen and ink
8½ × 10½ inches · 215 × 267 mm
Signed: *JW RA*

LITERATURE: Nygren, 1976, p.70, repr. fig. 101

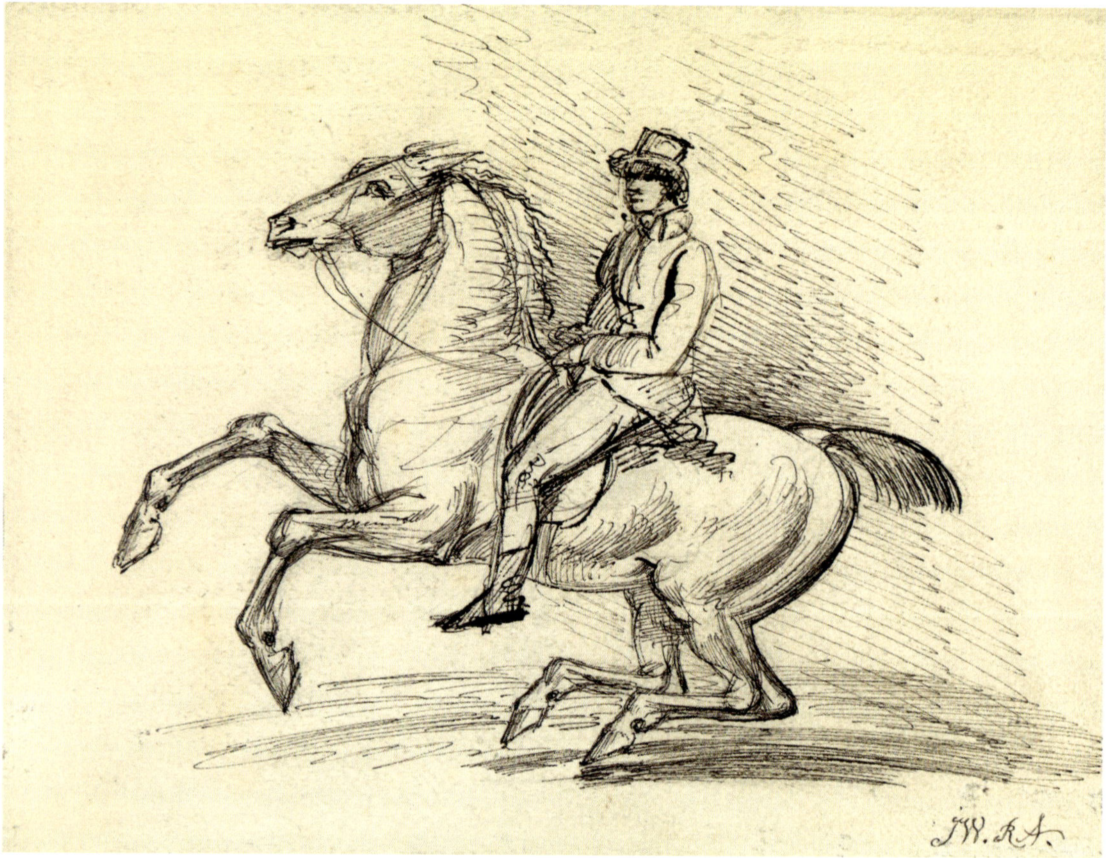

The pose seen here is based on an equestrian figure found in the North Frieze of the Elgin Marbles (xxxvii, 113–115). A similar drawing of a mounted figure, shown facing the other way is in Yale Center for British Art, New Haven. These drawings may be related to Ward's painting of *Sir Theophilus Levett and a favourite hunter* of 1817, also at the Yale Center for British Art. The portrait shows the landowner and politician Levett hunting on his estate at Wychnor Park. Levett was one of Ward's most important patrons and the portrait commission undoubtedly generated a number of preparatory studies. Our drawing and the Yale drawing show Levett's horse animatedly rearing, whilst the finished portrait shows him stationary, surveying his estate. The present ink study with its lively hatched lines and bold construction are reminiscent of the works of contemporary French draughtsman, such as Théodore Géricault.

46 THE COSSACK CLOAK

Pencil · 14⅜ × 9½ inches · 365 × 241 mm
Signed *JWD RA* and inscribed *Cossack cover / against rain / King Street*

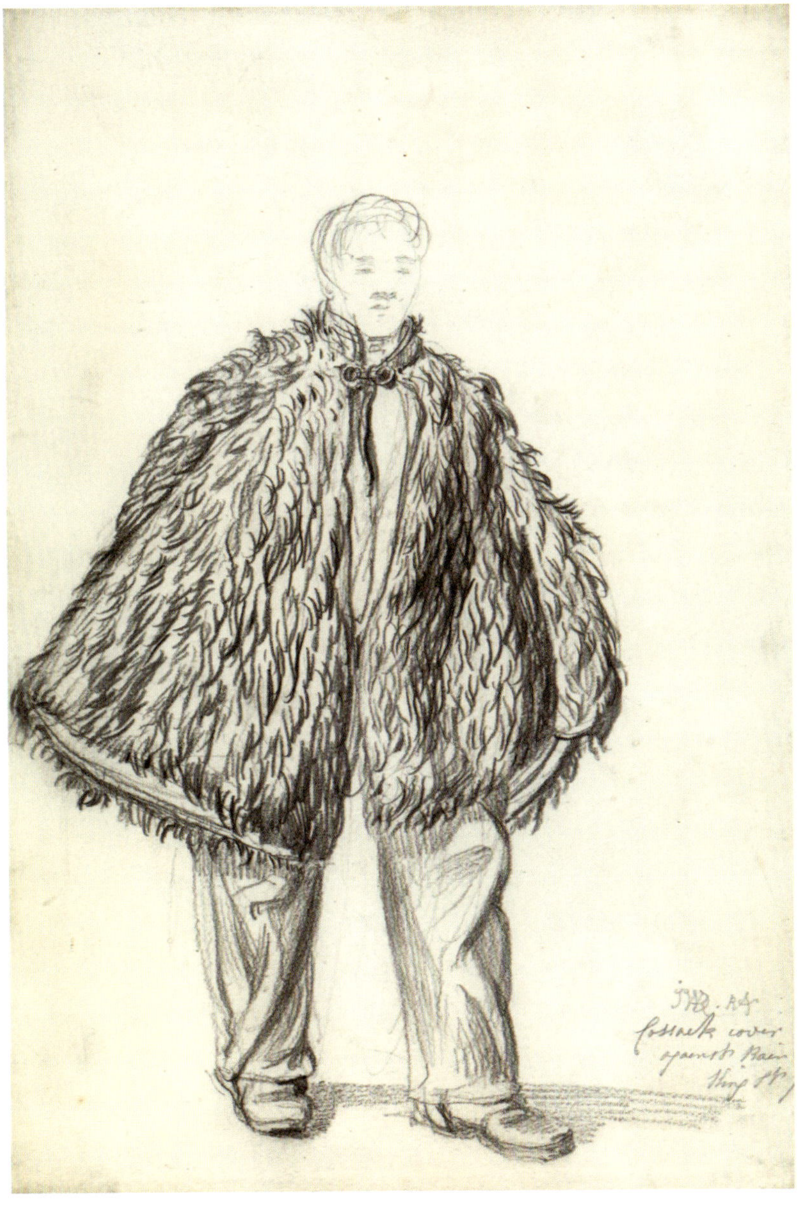

In the summer of 1814 London was captivated by the arrival of a Russian delegation headed by Tsar Alexander at the invitation of the Prince Regent. They formed part of the Allied Sovereign's Visit conducted between 6th and 27th June, following Napoleon's abdication after the signing of the First Treaty of Paris in May that year. King Frederick IV of Prussia, the Chancellor of Austria and the sovereigns of Sweden and various German States were invited to England, along with their generals and various events took place to mark the occasion, including a *levée* undertaken by the Russians.

Members of the Tsar's entourage stayed at the King Street barracks just north of Portman Square and their distinctive costume fascinated the population. In 1815 Ward exhibited *A Charger belonging to Count Platoff with Four Cossacks*, (collection, Duke of Northumberland, Alnwick Castle) at the Royal Academy. Ward was clearly as captivated by the Russians as his contemporaries, for he produced a number of detailed portrait drawings of members of the delegation from life, such as the present drawing. Others include two portrait drawings of *Gregory Yelloserf*, (Yale Center for British Art, New Haven and Private collection) as well as two studies of *Tarmorfait Carborlof*, one also in the Fitzwilliam Museum, Cambridge and the other in the Ashmolean Museum, Oxford.

47 A DRUMMER WOMAN AND A FIGURE OF A SOLDIER

Pencil · 7¼ × 4½ inches · 182 × 115 mm
Signed: *JWD RA*

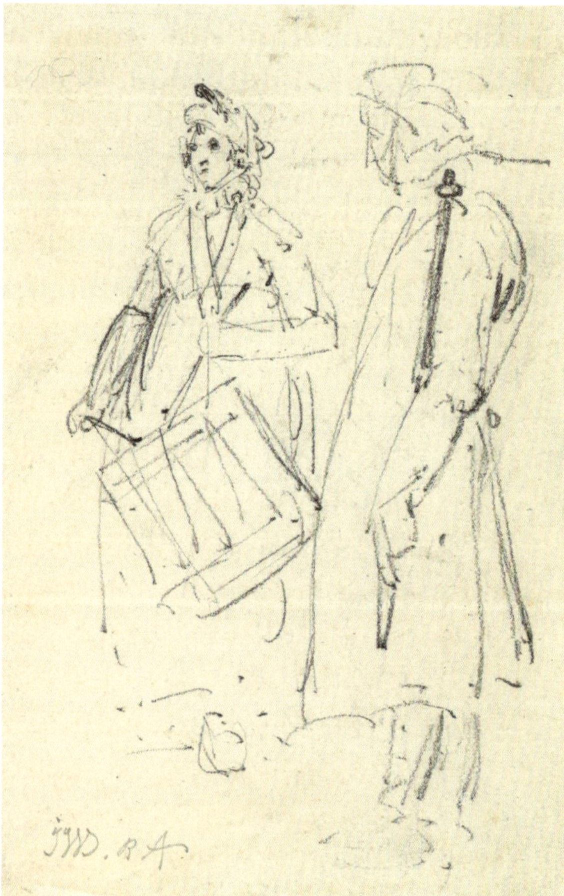

The present study appears to show a female drummer. Whilst women were commonly camp followers at this time, there are, somewhat rarely, women who served in the ranks. Whether this is in fact a rare image of one such woman is uncertain.

48 A SEATED FIGURE

Pencil and white chalk
10⅞ × 7¾ inches · 277 × 196 mm
Signed: *JW*

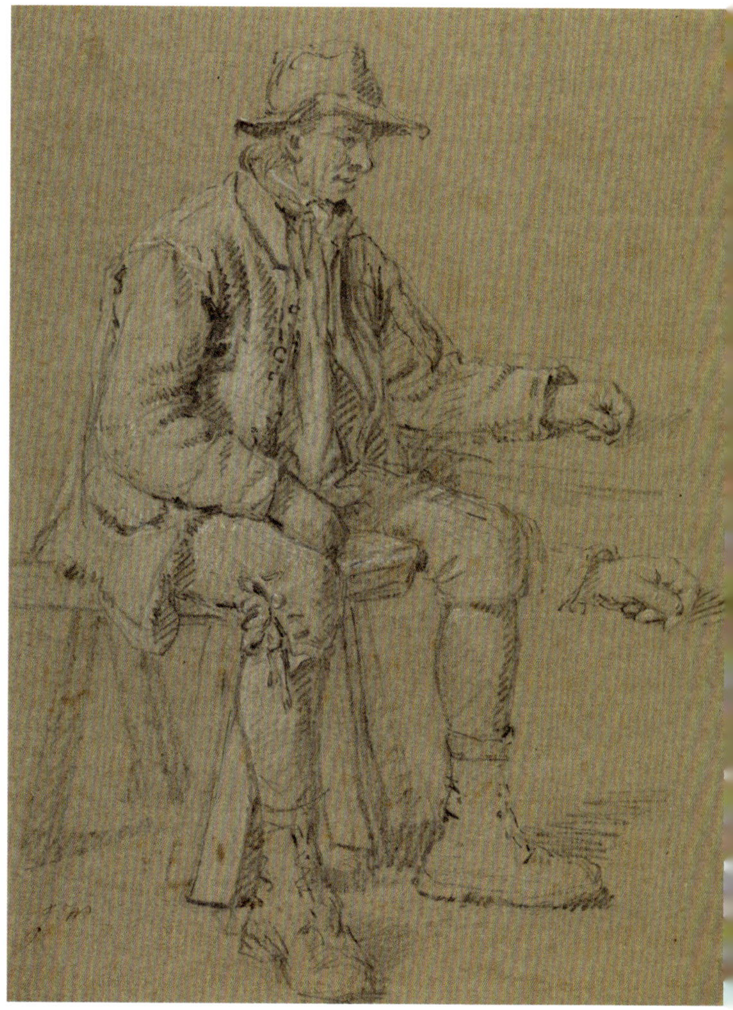

49 JOSEPH WITTINGHAM, A MURDERER

Pencil · 5⅝ × 4⅛ inches · 143 × 104 mm
Signed *JWD RA* and also inscribed verso: *Joseph Willingham / was in a degree insane, but was / allowed with fetters on, to work in the / Lead Mines at Castleton in the / Peake Derby shire, in a fit of / phrensy he had killed a man. His expression and manner marked / great depression.*

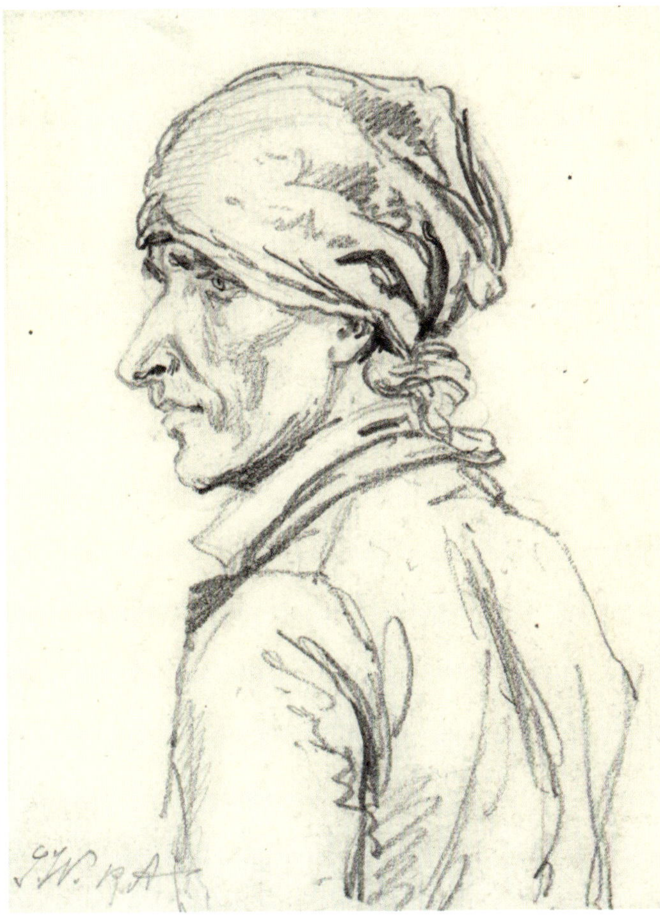

Given Ward's interest in the physiognomy and the human form, the opportunity to depict a convicted criminal must have appealed to him. The over-riding emotion in the present drawing is one of sympathy, a feeling that is reinforced by the inscription on the verso of the sheet. Willingham is shown as a dignified, almost noble figure by Ward. Nygren (Nygren, 1976, p.94) has pointed out that, like Géricault, Ward displayed a fascination for the curious or atypical and he made visits to an asylum kept by a priest, Dr Woody, at Tamworth.

50 I WAS A STRANGER AND YE TOOK ME IN

Oil on panel
7¾ × 10 inches · 197 × 254 mm
Signed *JW RA* and inscribed *I was a stranger / and ye took me in!* by the artist on a label on the verso and also branded *IWRA*

LITERATURE: Nygren, 1976, p.218, repr. fig. 234

EXHIBITED: London, Plymouth, Newcastle-upon-Tyne, Leeds & Cardiff, Arts Council exhibition, *James Ward 1769–1859*, 1960, no.53.

A religious man, Ward apparently knew the *Bible* and Bunyan's *Pilgrim's Progress* by heart. He believed that his ability to paint was a gift from God and therefore something he should always strive to use to the utmost of his abilities. The title of this painting of the 1840s is taken from the Gospel of Matthew (ch. 25 v 35): 'For I was an hungry, and ye gave me meat: I was thirsty, and ye gave me drink: I was a stranger, and ye took me in'. It was common in this period to append Bible quotations to genre scenes and the verses from Matthew 25 were frequently added to rustic scenes. The popularity of such scenes may have prompted Ward to produce the current picture, which was derived from an earlier life study and is one which Ward describes as having occured with his wife and their servant Pegg. A chalk drawing on blue paper of the same subject is inscribed *Samuel Fry Tytherton* and dated 1807. Tytherton in Wiltshire was the home of Ward's early patron, the animal breeder Thomas Crook.

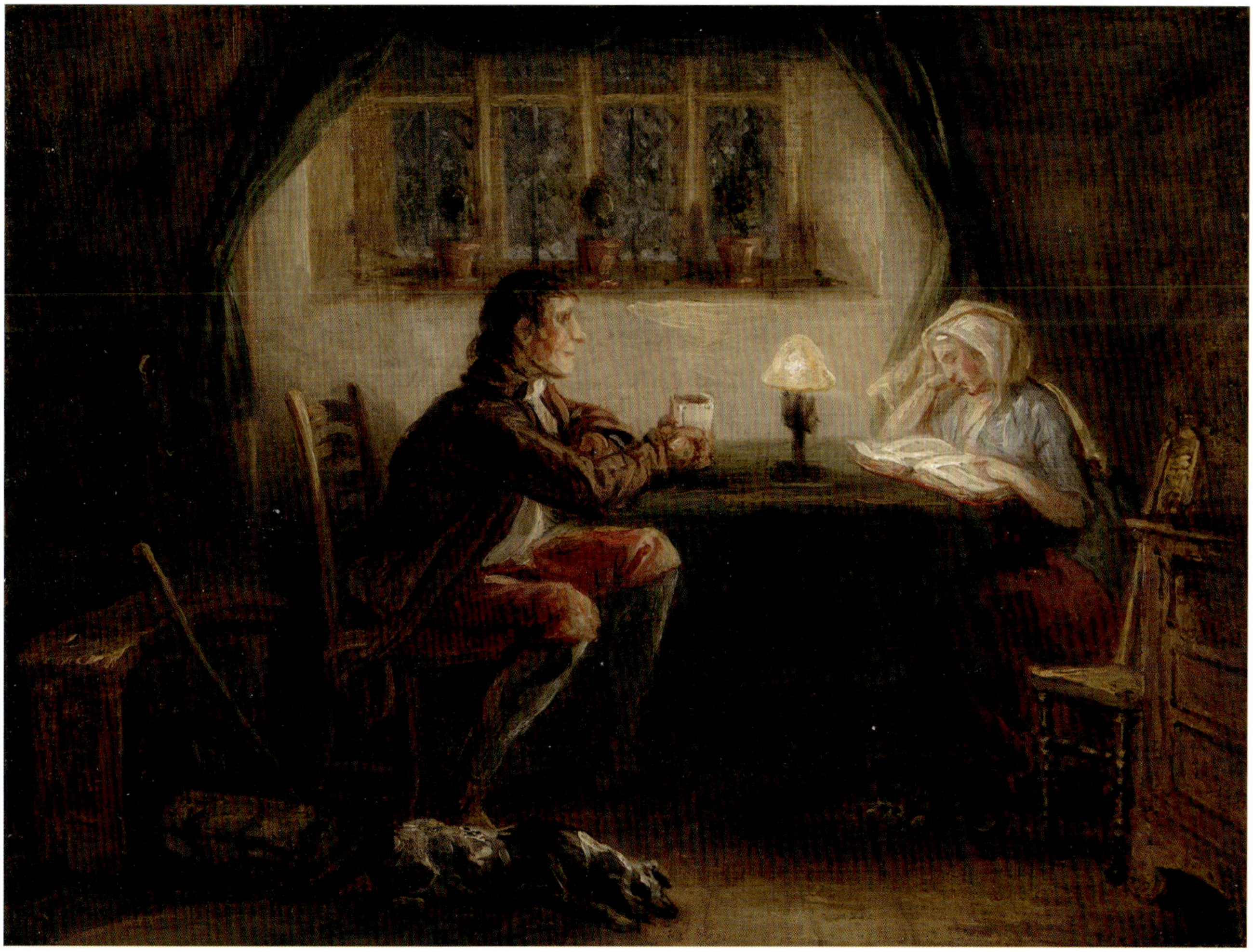

51 A SLEEPING FIGURE

Pencil · 7⅜ × 7¼ inches · 187 × 184 mm
Signed: *JWD RA*

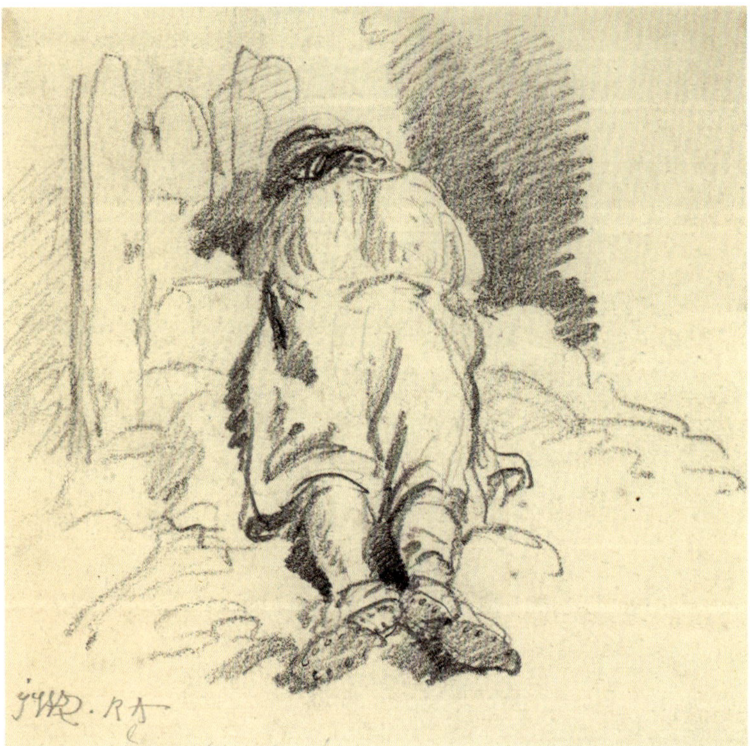

This rapidly handled drawing suggests that it must have been executed *ad vivum*. Ward probably came across the sleeping figure whilst on one of his sketching trips. There is a similar study of a sleeping figure in the Fitzwilliam Museum, Cambridge. The inclusion of such minute details as the nails on the bottoms of the subject's shoes adds to the sense of realism.

52 A MAN TYING UP A ROPE

Pencil · 7⅜ × 4¾ inches · 187 × 120 mm
Signed twice *JW* and *JWD RA* and inscribed: *land colour'd / Hole Deal*

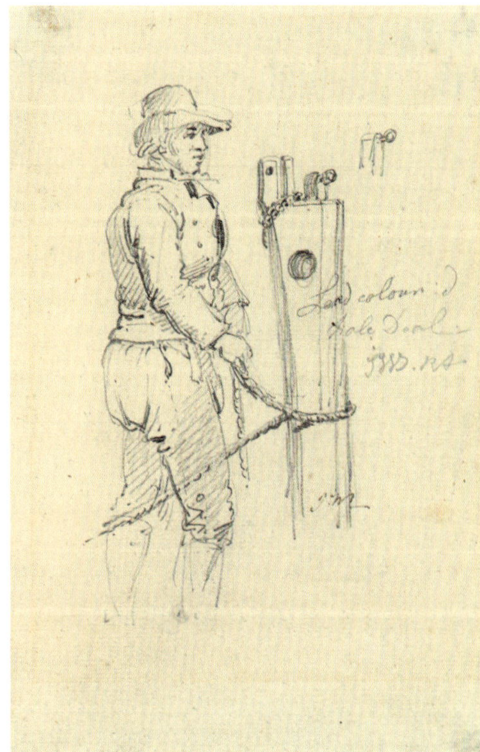

This drawing, which possibly shows a man tying up a boat, is characteristic of the type of studies Ward made on sketching trips throughout his career. The present work bears two sets of initials, one set probably inscribed when the drawing was executed and the one set inscribed at a later date when Ward was thinking of disposing of all remaining works to fund an annuity.

53 A SHEPHERD WITH HIS SHEEP IN A PEN

Pencil · 5 × 6¾ inches · 128 × 172 mm
Signed: *JWD RA*

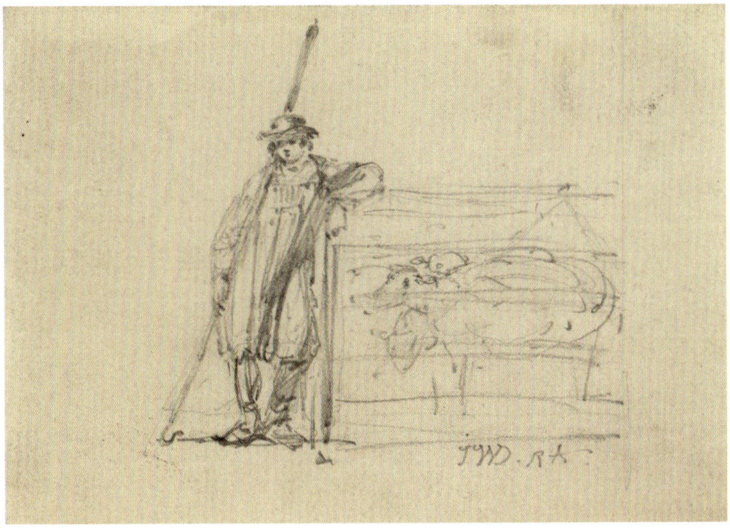

From his earliest work for the Board of Agriculture Ward had a fascination with the process of agricultural life and of livestock in particular. The freedom of handling suggests that this was drawn from life, the emphasis is clearly on the more defined figure of the shepherd whilst the more schematic study of the sheep serves to enlarge the composition and locate the figure.

This drawing of *c.*1802–07 is a good example of how Ward used his archive of sketches. Ward introduced the standing figure seen here into his 1829 painting of *Sheep Shearing and Salving* (Birmingham Museums and Art Gallery)

54 A SHEET OF FIGURE STUDIES

Pencil · 6⅝ × 4½ inches · 168 × 114 mm
Signed: *JW*

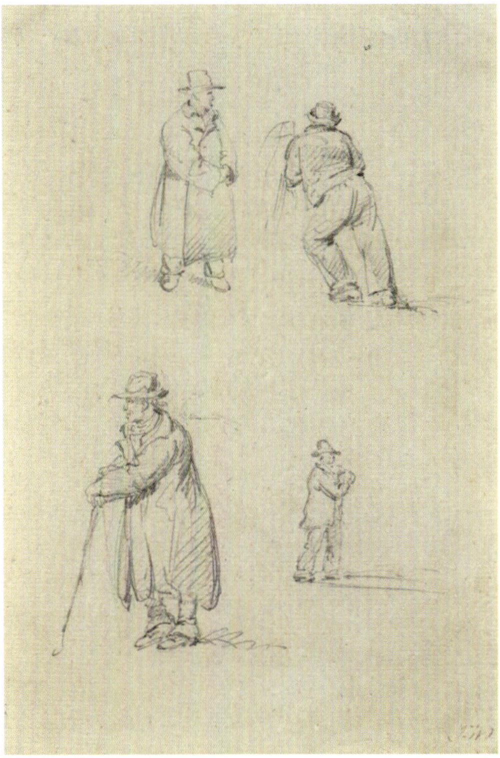

This sheet of rapidly executed studies was probably made by Ward on one of his frequently sketching trips. Ward was particularly interested in the customs and activities of agricultural workers. Nygren has recently pointed out that these small figure studies are similar to those created by W.H. Pyne and published in his various books. Pyne was a member of the drawing club of which Ward was also a member in the early years of the century.

III
Ward and the Civil War

Writing to his patron, the great collector Sir John Leicester, Ward reported in August 1824 that Lord Northwick:

> *has offered me 500 Guineas to paint him a Battle in the time of Cromwell, of the same size treated in any way I please — I like the thing mightily, there is variety of colour, stuffs, Leathers, armour, Beards, strong Horses, and other good matters at that period. There are also some broad brown hard faces — with rude expression &c &c but after all what has the little animal painter to do with all this combination of active Humanity. (Letter to Sir John Leicester, August 12 1824, in Nygren, 2013, p.172.)*

The present catalogue contains a number of studies which demonstrate Ward's evident delight in 'the variety' of seventeenth-century costume and armour and his determination to transform from the 'little animal painter' into an historical master.

The subject of the English Civil War held enormous appeal during the early decades of the nineteenth century not only in Britain, but also in France where historians such as François-René Chateubriand drew parallels with the French Revolution. In 1813 Sir Walter Scott published his *Rokeby*, a poem set in Yorkshire immediately after the Battle of Marston Moor. It was hugely successful with 10,000 copies sold within the first three months of publication. In 1831 J.M.W. Turner worked on illustrations to a revised edition of the poem with Scott and in the same year that Ward completed his canvas for Northwick, Scott produced another Civil War work, *Woodstock or the Cavalier: A Tale of the Year Sixteen Hundred and Fifty-one*. In France the following year, Victor Hugo published his play, *Cromwell,* and a decade later Paul Delaroche, who had become known for his paintings of English history, exhibited *Charles I insulted by Cromwell's Soldiers*. He was still engaged by the subject over a decade later, when in 1849 he painted *Cromwell before the coffin of Charles I*, a theme also treated by Eugène Delacroix.

Ward's commission from Lord Northwick therefore gave Ward the opportunity to handle not only a major historical subject, but one that was at the height of popularity amongst contemporaries. Ward in fact exhibited two paintings with Civil War subjects at the Royal Academy: *The Battle near Boston*, in 1826 (23) and *The Discomfiture of Charles II at Worcester*, 1847 (10). Our group of studies of armour, military uniforms and weapons give us an extraordinary insight into the Ward's scrupulous working methods as he prepared to become a serious historical painter. He went to great lengths to ensure historical accuracy. An inscription on two of the drawings (cats.64 A and 66) refer to Sir Samuel Meyrick (1783–1848), a noted antiquarian and leading specialist on historical arms and armour who was frequently consulted by artists. In 1824 Meyrick published his three volume *Critical enquiry into antient armour*, although as these drawings do not relate to specific plates, it seems likely Ward had access to Meyrick's collection.

Three other drawings in this group are based on an earlier publication, Sir Francis Grose's *A treatise on Ancient Armour and Weapons illustrated by plates taken from the Original Armour in the Tower of London and other Arsenals, Museums and Cabinets*, published in 1786. Others appear to have been drawn from life, sketched whilst staying with patrons, or on his sketching tours, such as the study of *Sir John Gell's doublet* made when Ward was visiting Hopton Hall in Derbyshire (cat.71) and *Cromwellian Boots* (cat.70) which are inscribed: 'Haddon Hall', the Derbyshire house of the dukes of Rutland.

55 STUDY FOR 'THE DISCOMFITURE OF CHARLES II AT THE BATTLE OF WORCESTER'

Oil on panel
5¼ × 7½ inches · 134 × 190 mm
Signed with *IWRA* brand verso

LITERATURE: Nygren, 1976, p.247, repr. fig. 271

EXHIBITED: London, Plymouth, Newcastle-upon-Tyne, Leeds & Cardiff, Arts Council exhibition, *James Ward 1769–1859*, 1960, no.30

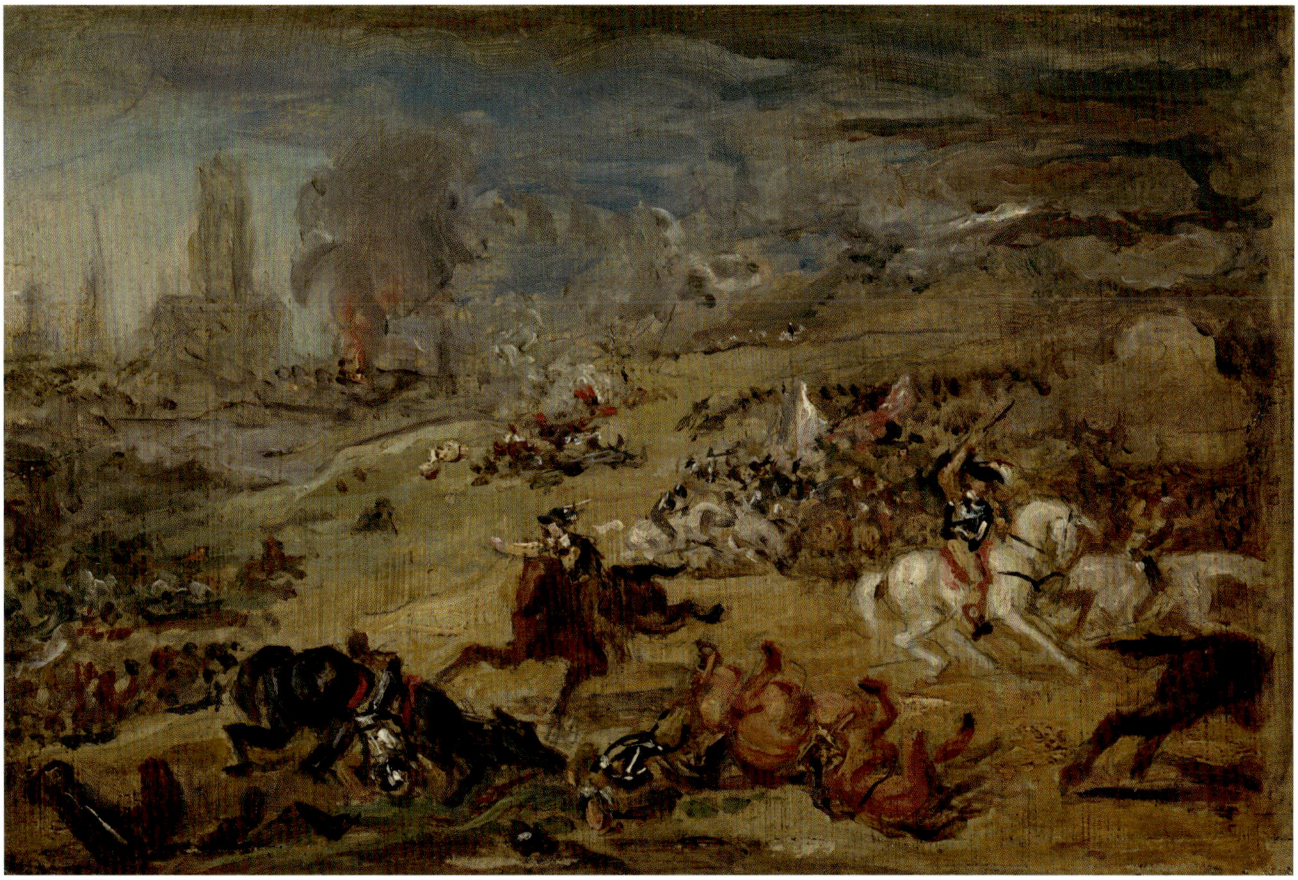

This rapidly executed oil sketch is a study for Ward's painting *The Discomfiture of Charles II at the Battle of Worcester*, exhibited at the Royal Academy in 1847 (10). It depicts the battle of Worcester, which took place in 1651 between Cromwell's New Model Army and the Royalist forces of Charles II. The painting shows the tower of Worcester cathedral prominently on the horizon, Charles II used the cathedral tower as a vantage point to view the battlefield and command his troops. Ward depicts a number of moments from the battle; in the foreground the Parliamentarian General John Lambert is shown just after his horse was shot from under him, whilst in the background Ward shows the fight for the King's standard. The mounted figure to the right seems likely to be Oliver Cromwell. Ward's picture is close in composition to another depiction of *The Battle of Worcester* by the equestrian painter Thomas Woodward, shown at the Royal Academy in 1837 (505) and now in Worcester City Art Gallery.

56 A SKIRMISH

Pen and ink · 7⅛ × 8⅝ inches · 182 × 219 mm
Signed: *JWD RA*

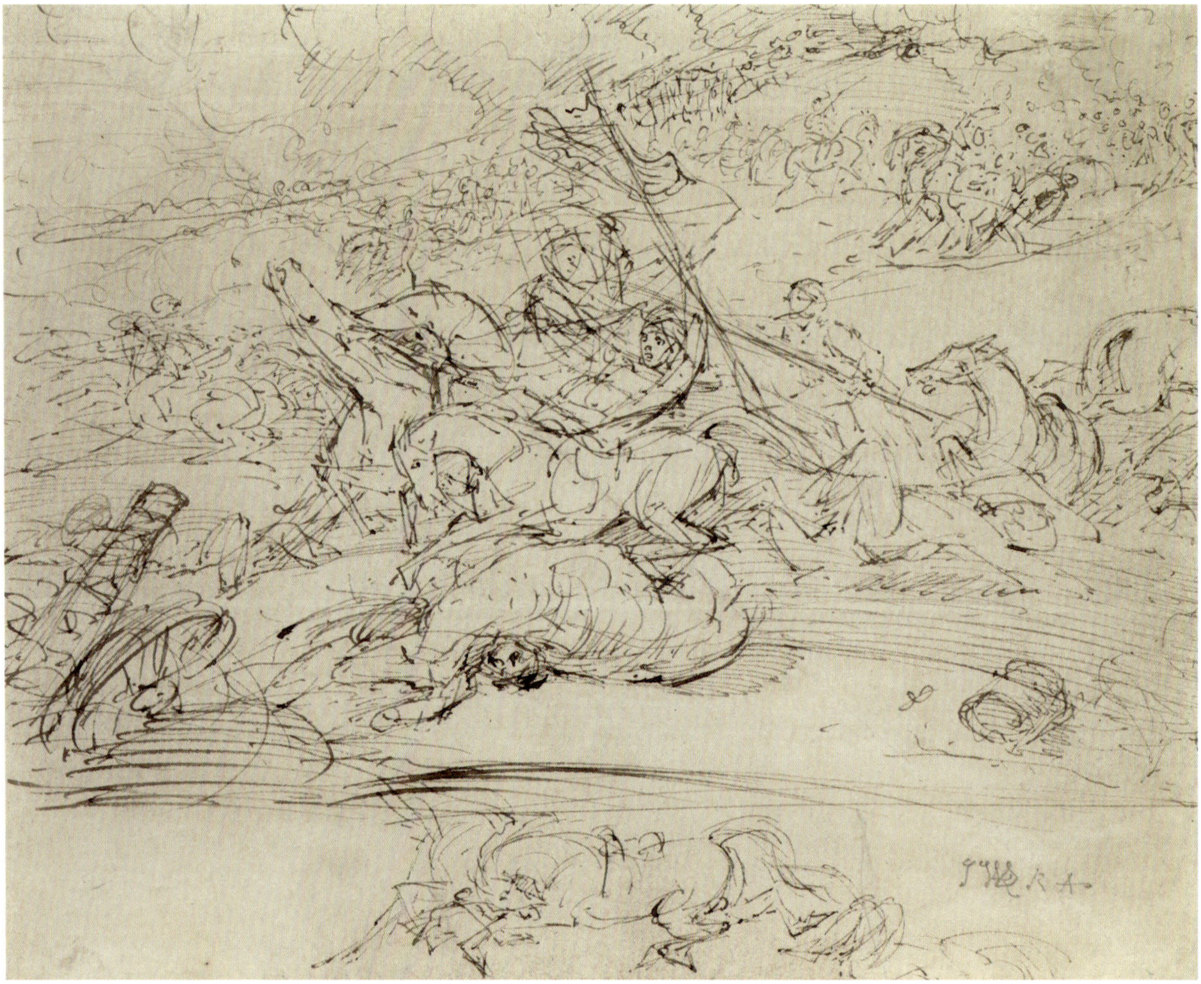

This complexly rendered pen and ink study seems to have been made in preparation for a battle composition. Ward has communicated the confusion of the battle in the mesh of ink lines. Ward completed a number of studies of cavalry skirmishes although it is not precisely clear which composition the present sheet relates to.

57 STUDIES FOR THE 'DISCOMFITURE OF CHARLES II AT THE BATTLE OF WORCESTER'

Pencil · 7½ × 8⅞ inches · 191 × 226 mm
Signed: *JWD RA*

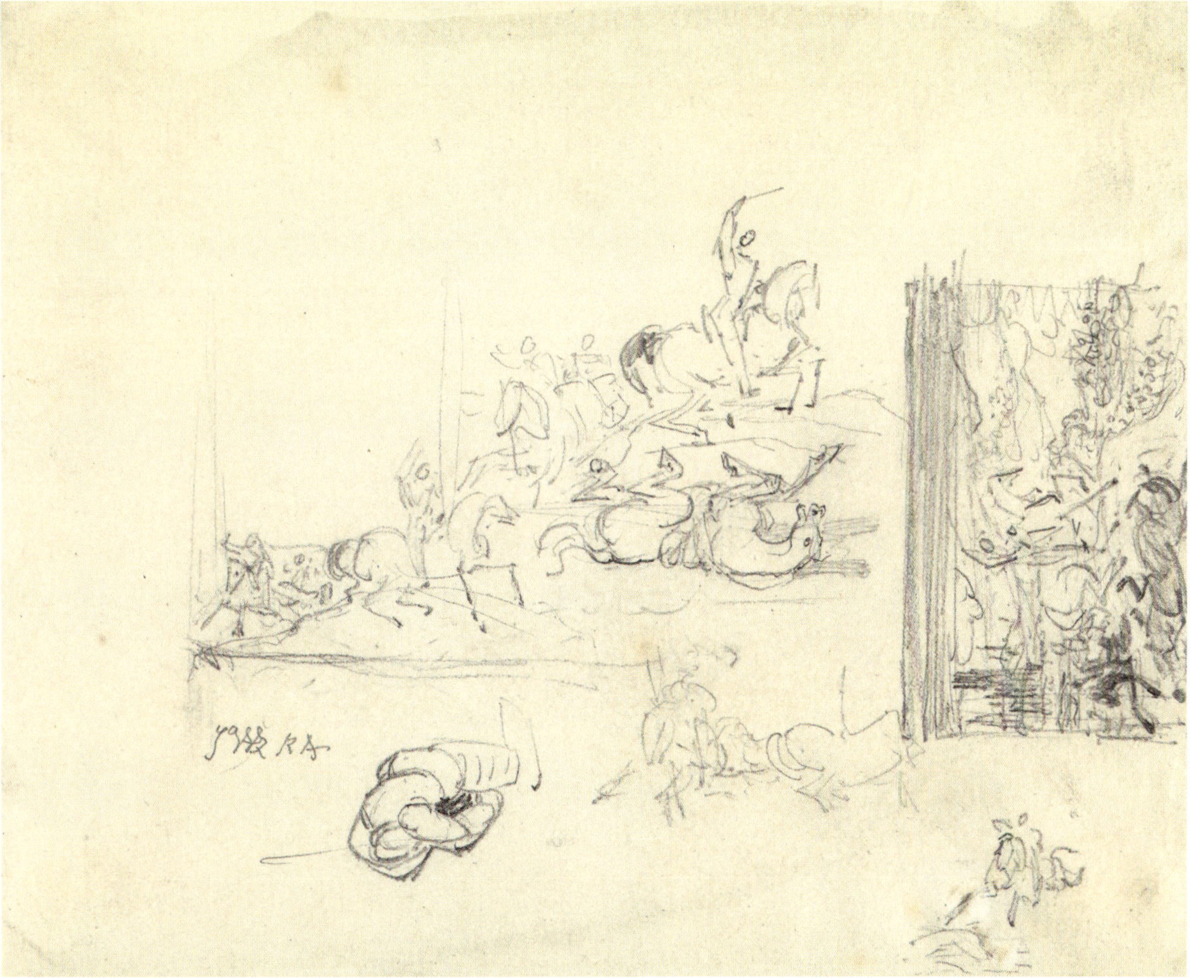

This sheet of fluid compositional studies all relate to Ward's painting *The Discomfiture of Charles II at the Battle of Worcester*, which was exhibited at the Royal Academy in 1847 (10). This sheet clearly demonstrates the artist's thought process when working on a complex composition as well as his ability to render in rapid sketches an exploration of possible compositional arrangements. The oil study for the final composition is cat.55.

58 STUDY FOR THE 'BATTLE NEAR BOSTON': THE CENTRAL MELEE BEHIND CROMWELL

Pencil · 4½ × 7 inches · 114 × 178 mm
Signed: *JWD RA*

EXHIBITED: London, Plymouth, Newcastle-upon-Tyne, Leeds & Cardiff, Arts Council exhibition, *James Ward 1769–1859*, 1960, no.88 [the dimensions given in the catalogue are an error]

This is a preparatory study for the figures immediately to the left of Cromwell in the *Battle near Boston*, which was commissioned by Lord Northwick and exhibited at the Royal Academy in 1826 (23). A near full-scale study (25¼ × 37¼ inches) in oils for the composition is in the Cromwell Museum, Huntingdon.

The fluidity and elegance of line used to depict the horses in contrast with the much more angular lines used to depict the figures in armour creates a dynamic drawing full of energy and power. The light and sense of movement in the intertwined twisting figures of the horses are reminiscent of the work of Rubens, an artist who had a profound effect on Ward. The commission from Northwick was an important one, he was eventually paid £525 for the picture and Ward made a number of studies in preparation.

59 'SELF-POSSESSION': A MOUNTED KNIGHT

Oil on panel · 6¼ × 8 inches · 158 × 203 mm
Signed with *IWRA* brand on verso

LITERATURE: Nygren, 1976, p.233, repr. fig. 246

This study is of *Self-Possession*, one of the *Twenty Figures descriptive of the various Expressions, Actions and Character of the Horse* that Ward exhibited at Newman Street in 1841. In this series Ward attempted a summation of his art in an Aesopian vein: exploring man's spiritual and moral state through a carefully conceived series of horse paintings accompanied by verse. The poem for *Self-Possession* underlined the senseless pomp and pageantry associated with war by observing that it inevitably led to the grave.

The treatment of the mounted figure was evidently based on Van Dyck's equestrian portrait of Charles I. The similarity of the pose of the horse and the touches of red on the bridle, saddlecloth and the plume appear to indicate that this work is closely related to the pencil drawing with heraldic pennants (cat.60).

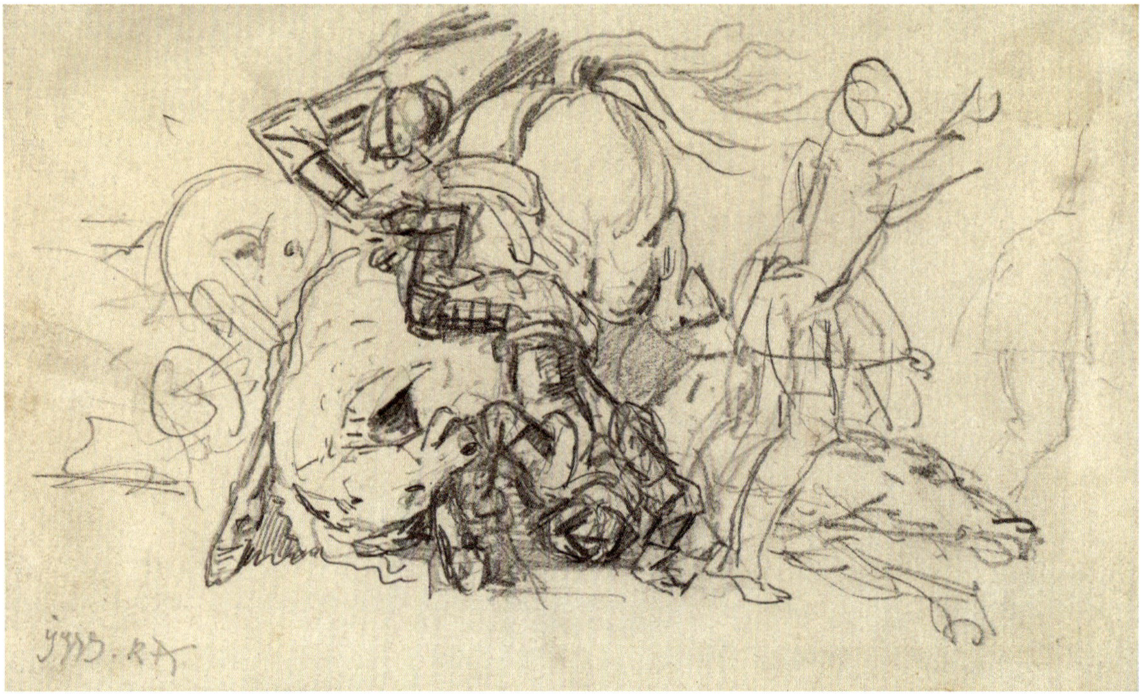

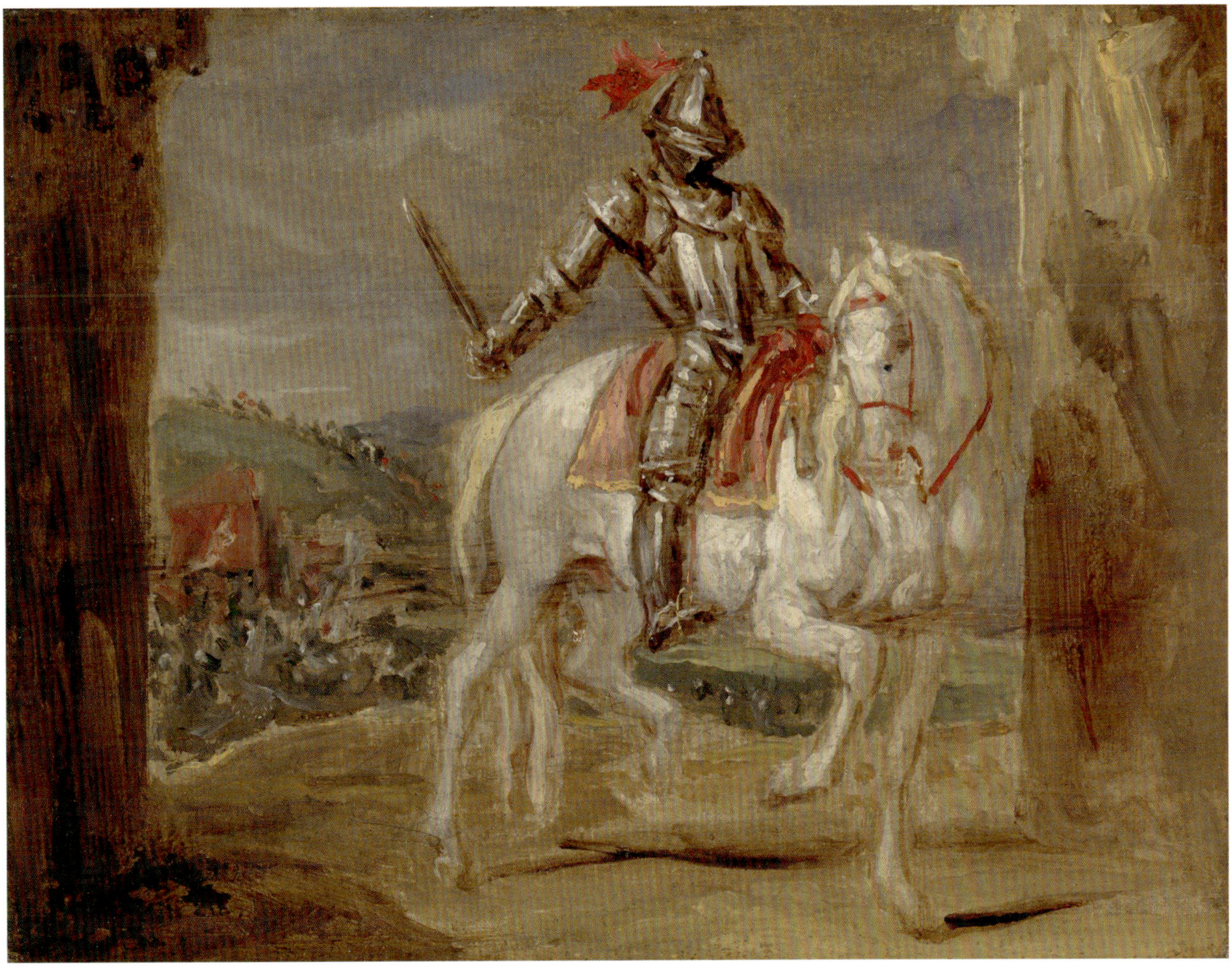

60 A MOUNTED KNIGHT IN FULL ARMOUR WITH HERALDIC PENNANTS

Pencil and watercolour · 7 × 10¼ inches · 179 × 260 mm
Signed JWD RA and extensively inscribed: *Gen'l Fairfax Cap. Henry Ireton Col. Ingoldsby / Same colours as Ireton / He had also a plain bright blue / with gold motto diagonal.*

The mounted figure appears to relate to the oil sketch: *Self-Possession* (cat.59). Sir Thomas Fairfax (1612–1671) was appointed Commander-in-Chief of the New Model Army in 1645. Under Fairfax the New Model Army suffered no defeats and in July 1647 his success was recognised when he was appointed Commander-in-Chief of all Parliaments Land Forces. Like many senior Parliamentarians, including General Monk, on the Restoration of the monarchy Fairfax managed to effect a pardon from Charles II and also supplied the horse that Charles II rode at his coronation.

Richard Ingoldsby (1617–1685), on the other hand, was far more politically motivated. He was a firm supporter of the Protectorate and was one of the signatories on Charles I's death warrant. However, on Richard Cromwell's deposition he became one of the most prominent of the Cromwell's former commanders to support the return of the monarchy. He managed to obtain a pardon from Charles II, by stating that Cromwell seized his hand and traced his signature on the warrant. Almost uniquely amongst the regicides he managed to retain the lands he had acquired under the Protectorate. He remained politically active during both Charles II and James IIs' reigns and was appointed a Knight of the Bath and a Gentleman to the King's Privy Chamber.

Henry Ireton (1611–1651) was a zealous Puritan and close friend and confident of Oliver Cromwell and married his eldest daughter Bridget. He was appointed a Commissioner of the High Court of Justice and was one of the most enthusiastic of the signatories on the King's death warrant. He proposed that all members of the newly-formed Council of State sign a declaration pledging their approval of the execution, the abolition of the monarchy and the House of Lords and their loyalty to the new regime. He was second in command to Cromwell on his Irish campaigns and, on Cromwell's return to England in 1650, was appointed commander of the Army in Ireland. On his death in Ireland in 1651, his body was returned to England where it lay in state at Westminster Abbey. Following the Restoration, his body was exhumed and hanged at Tyburn; his head displayed at Westminster for at least 24 years.

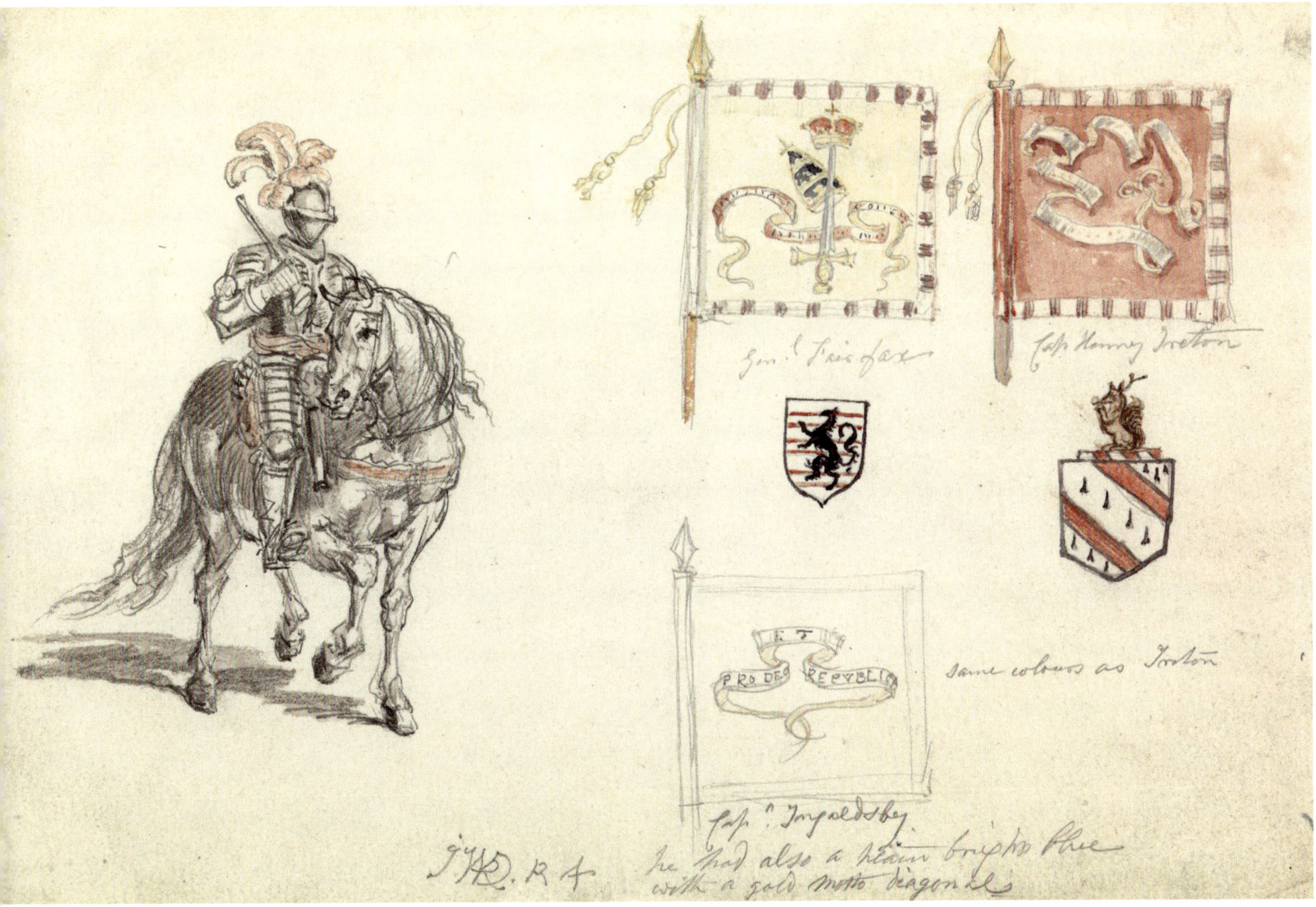
Genl Fairfax
Capt Henry Ireton
ET
PRO DEO REPUBLI
same colours as Ireton
Captn Ingoldsby
he had also a plain bright blue
with a gold motto diagonal

61 STUDIES OF ARMOUR

Pencil · 10¾ × 15 inches · 271 × 380 mm
Signed: *JWD RA*

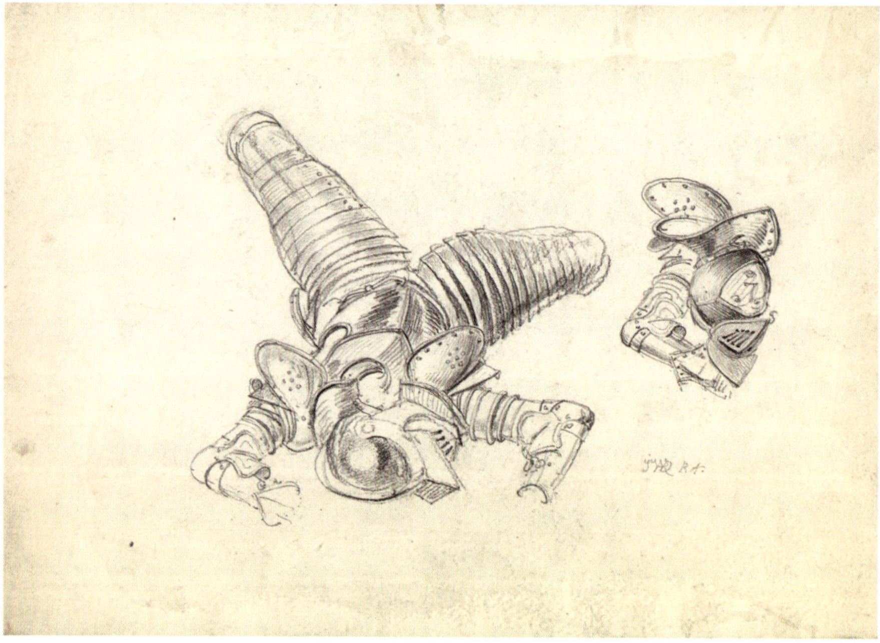

The highly detailed nature of these armour studies as well as the play of light and shadow on their surface, suggest that they were sketches drawn from actual examples.

62 A FIGURE IN ARMOUR, SEEN FROM BEHIND

Pencil · 8¾ × 8 inches · 222 × 203 mm
Signed *JWD RA* and inscribed with shorthand notes

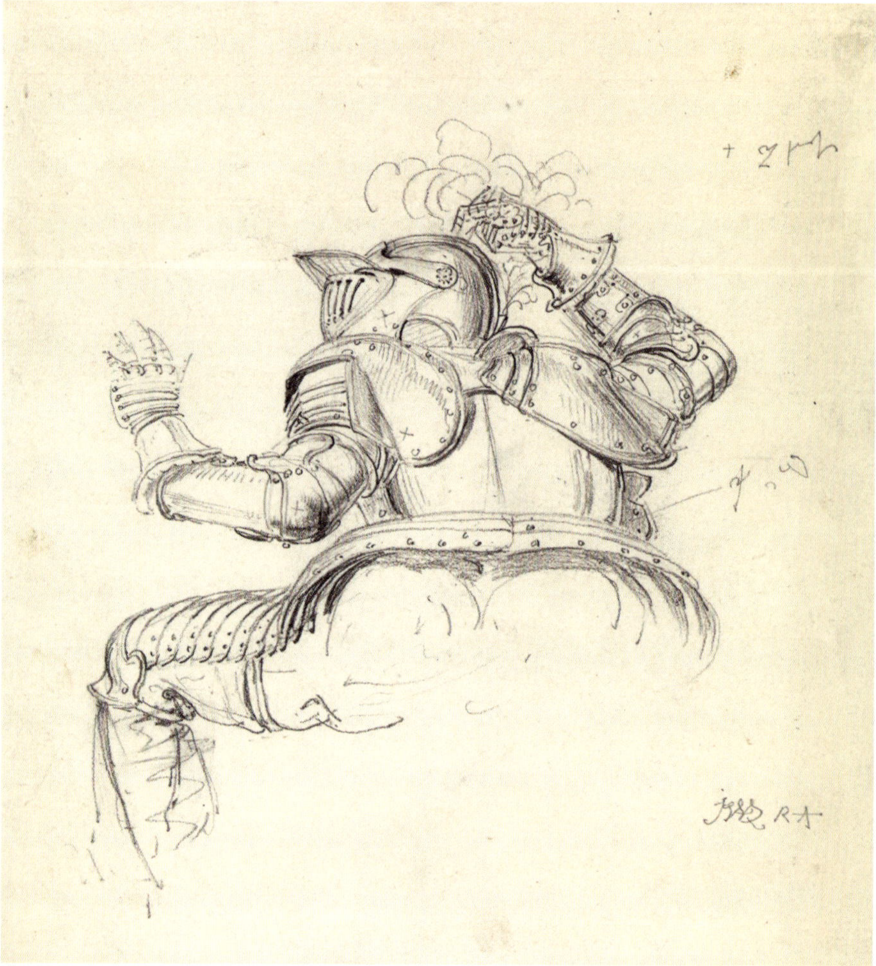

This highly detailed drawing appears to relate to the figure falling off the grey horse in the central group of Ward's *Battle near Boston, Lincolnshire*. The careful detailing, precise articulation of the armour and delicate hatching demonstrating the fall of light and shadow on the metal all suggest that this was a study made from life, possibly from a piece in the collection of Sir Samuel Meyrick.

63 STUDIES OF ARMOUR

Pencil on watermark paper: J Whatman Turkey Mill 1821
9¾ × 12 inches · 248 × 304 mm
Signed *JWD RA* and also inscribed in shorthand

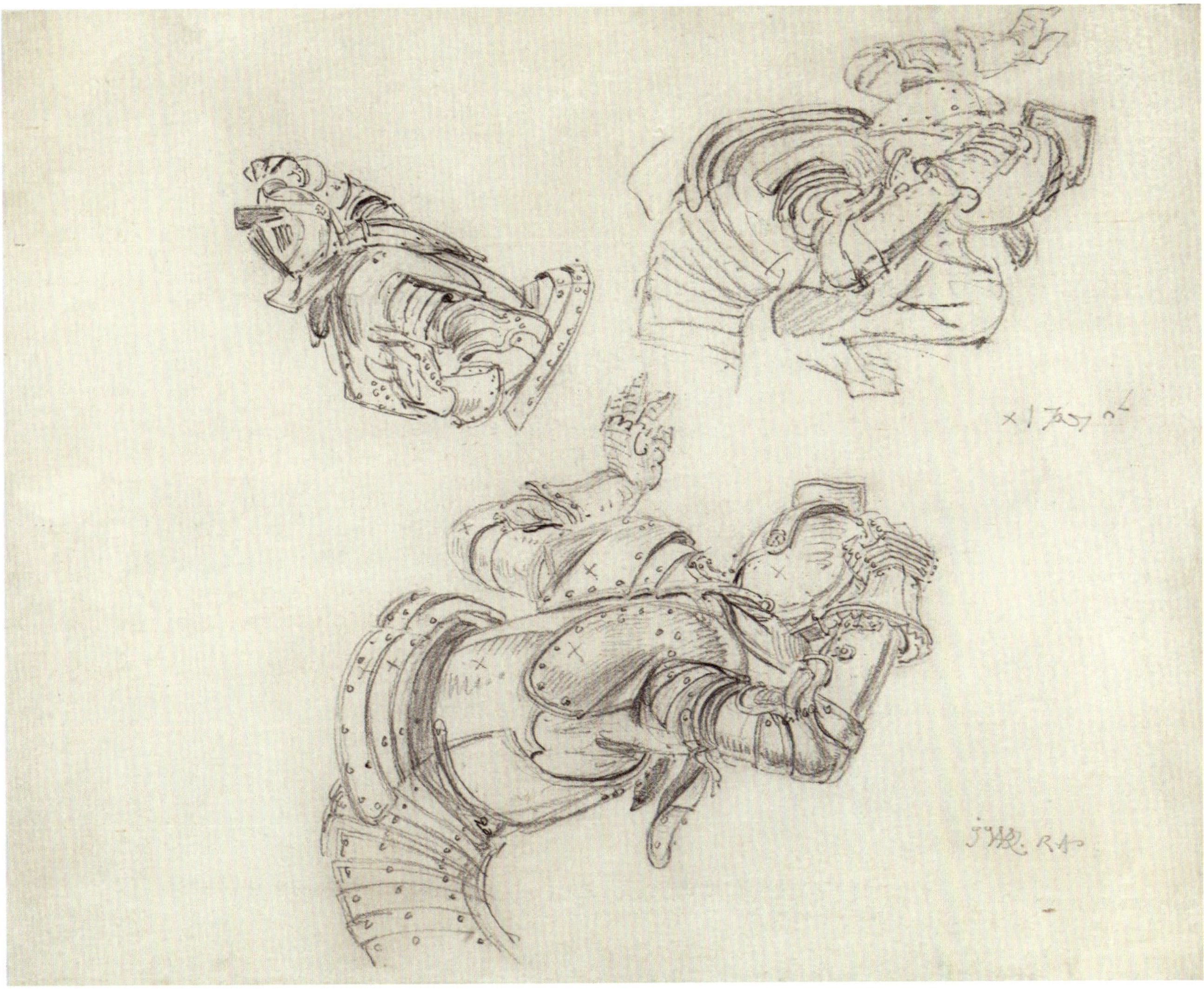

The present drawing, like cat.62, is a highly detailed and accurate study of armour, showing every rivet and joint with precision. This may be a study for one of the figures on the left hand side of *Battle near Boston, Lincolnshire.*

64 A DR MEYRICK'S BRASS FIGURE AND STUDIES OF PIKES

Pencil · 5½ × 9 inches · 140 × 229 mm
Signed *JWD RA* and inscribed: *Dr Meyrick's brass figure / Royalist / Republican / Charles / Time of James Ist / or Elizabeth*

64 B STUDY OF A SWORD USED AT THE BATTLE OF WORCESTER

Pencil · 5⅜ × 8¾ inches · 136 × 222 mm
Signed *JWD RA* and inscribed: *Sword used at the Battle of Worcester found in a farmhouse* and *both sides alike*

This sheet of studies confirms that Ward had access to the collection of the antiquarian and expert on arms and amour, showing as it does 'Dr Meyrick's brass figure' along with the profiles of three different pikes from the early seventeenth-century.

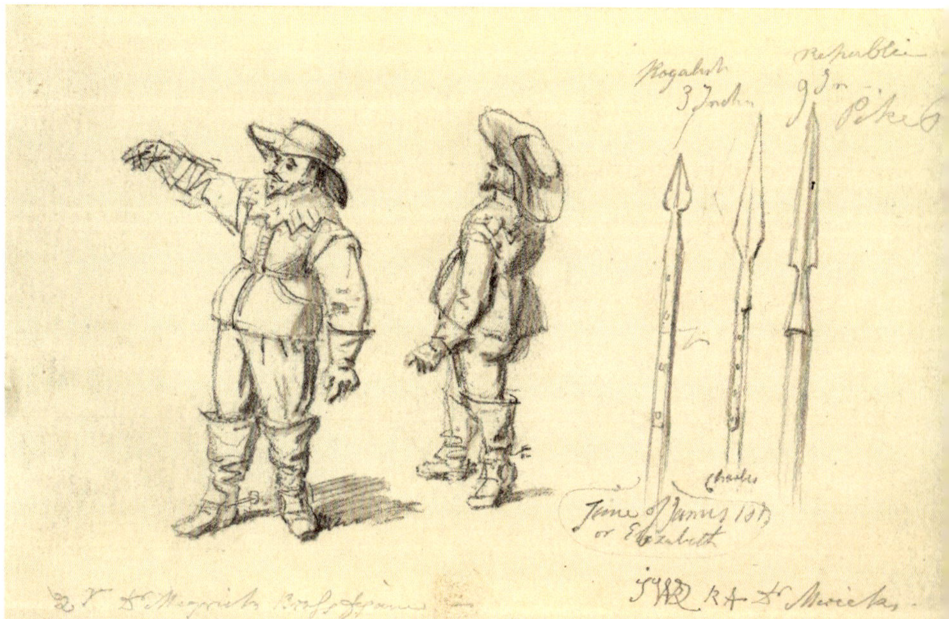

The inscription indicates that this sword was studied from life rather than based on an illustration. It is likely that in contrast to the other Civil War studies this sheet relates directly to Ward's painting of the *Battle of Worcester* made in the 1840s.

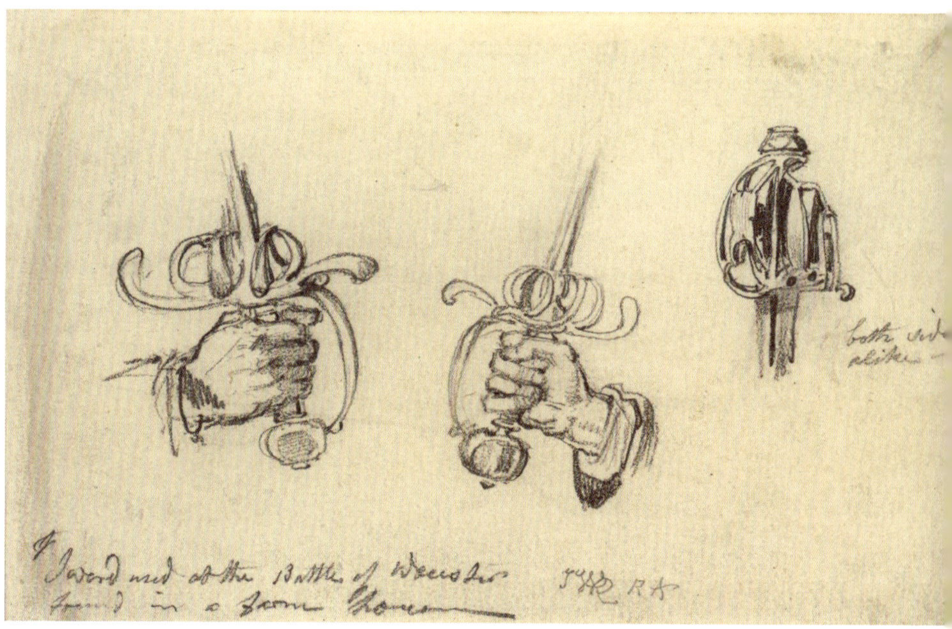

65 STUDIES OF GENERAL DAVID LESLIE AND OF A BREASTPLATE

Pencil · $5\frac{3}{8} \times 8\frac{5}{8}$ inches · 137×220 mm
Signed *JWD RA* and inscribed with artist's shorthand and further inscribed *Gen. Lesley*

The sketch of David Leslie, later Lord Newark, who commanded the Scottish cavalry at the battle of Worcester, is derived from an engraving of the sitter. The other studies show examples of engraved seventeenth-century armour.

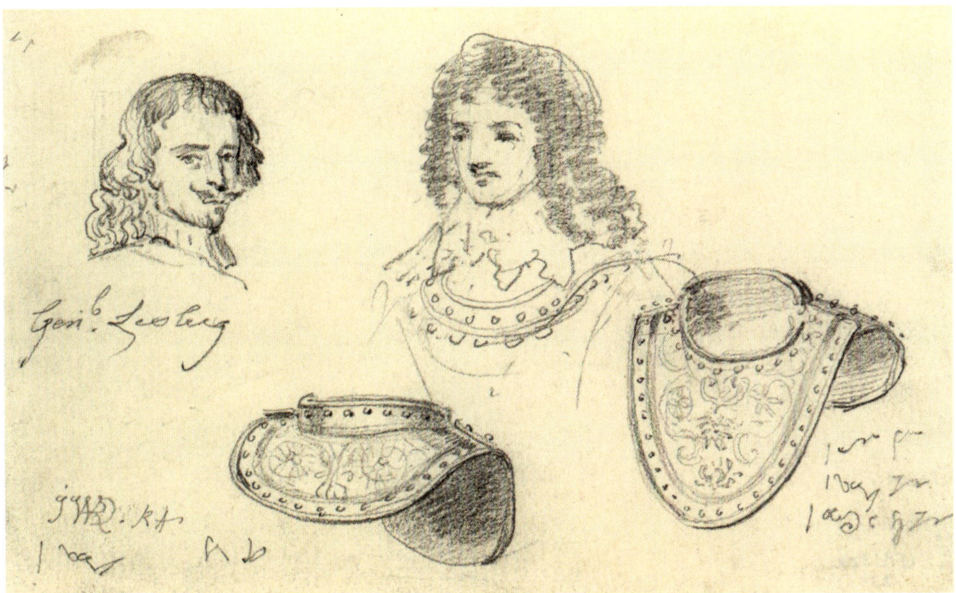

66 STUDIES OF ARMOUR

Pencil and watercolour
$7 \times 10\frac{1}{2}$ inches · 178×267 mm
Signed *JWD RA* and extensively inscribed and dated: *Pike man's courselet called a corselet / Dr Mayrick* [*sic*] *1824* also further inscribed in shorthand

LITERATURE: Nygren, 1976, p.171, repr. fig. 192

EXHIBITED: London, Plymouth, Newcastle-upon-Tyne, Leeds & Cardiff, Arts Council exhibition, *James Ward 1769–1859*, 1960, no.87.

This fine sheet of watercolour and pencil studies of seventeenth-century armour was made by Ward in preparation for his painting *Battle near Boston*. Several of the studies seem to have been taken from Samuel Meyrick's *Critical enquiry into antient armour*, published in 1824.

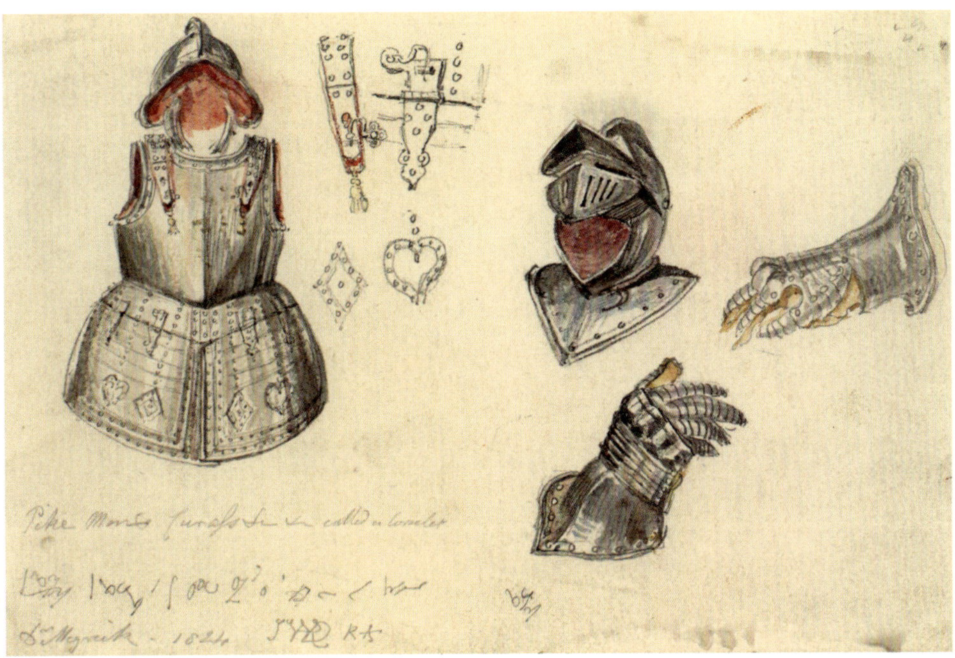

67 STUDIES OF CIVIL WAR ARMOUR

Pencil and brown wash
7 × 10½ inches · 178 × 267 mm
Signed *JWD RA* dated and variously inscribed with notes including: *Time of Cromwell / Time of Charles I / Gross ... 1824*

The various pieces of armour depicted here are all from plates in Francis Grose's *A treatise on ancient armour and weapons, illustrated by plates taken from the original armour in the tower of London, and other arsenals, museums, and cabinets*, published in 1786. The top row of studies (from left to right) are based on plate 7, no.5; plate 11, no.3; plate 17, nos. 1 and 2. The four studies along the bottom of the sheet (from left to right) all relate to images in the treatise, apart from the small helmet to the left of the coat which is the only piece of armour in cats. 67–69 that cannot be immediately identified with Grose's treatise. The other three are taken from plate 18 and plate 39, no.1. The helmet and corselet depicted at the bottom left were illustrated in Grose with the helmet resting on the corselet, whereas Ward has separated them.

68 STUDIES OF HELMETS

Pencil and brown wash
7 × 10¼ inches · 178 × 260 mm
Signed *JWD RA*, dated 1824 and variously inscribed with notes and the artist's shorthand, including *Grose's armour / pl. 5 no.1.2. time of Cromwell / no 3.4 / Cuirassier's helmet / time of Charles 2nd / time Charles 1st / pl.7 no 1.2 / Pot helmet of the Infantry / cavalry*

The various helmets on this sheet, taken from Francis Grose's treatise, were all in the collection at the Tower of London. The top three helmets (from left to right) are based on plate 5, nos. 1, 2 and 3. The three bottom helmets (from left to right) relate to plate 7, nos. 1 and 2 and plate 5, no.4. The bottom left and centre helmets are 'iron hats called pots, said to be taken from the French in the time of King Charles 1.' The bottom right helmet is shown sitting on a wooden stand in Grose's illustration but Ward chose to depict it without, perhaps to make it more naturalistic.

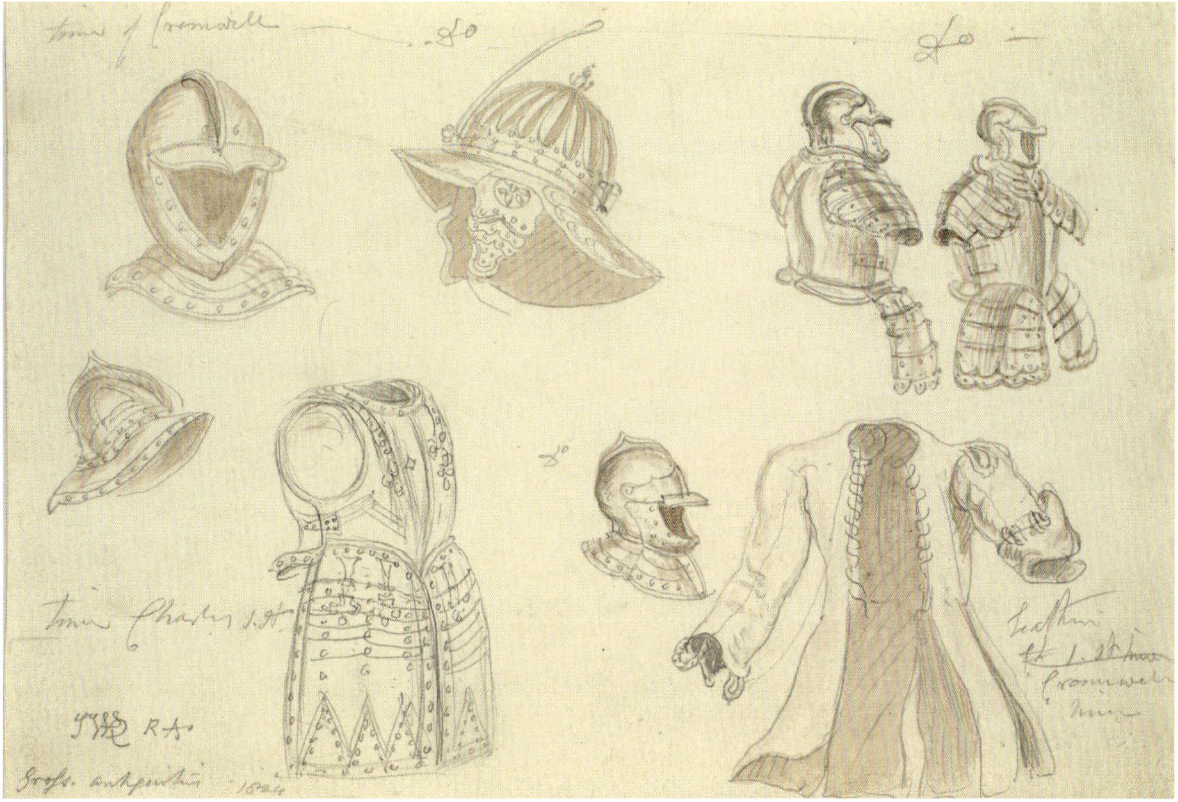
time of Cromwell
time Charles I st
Cromwell
time

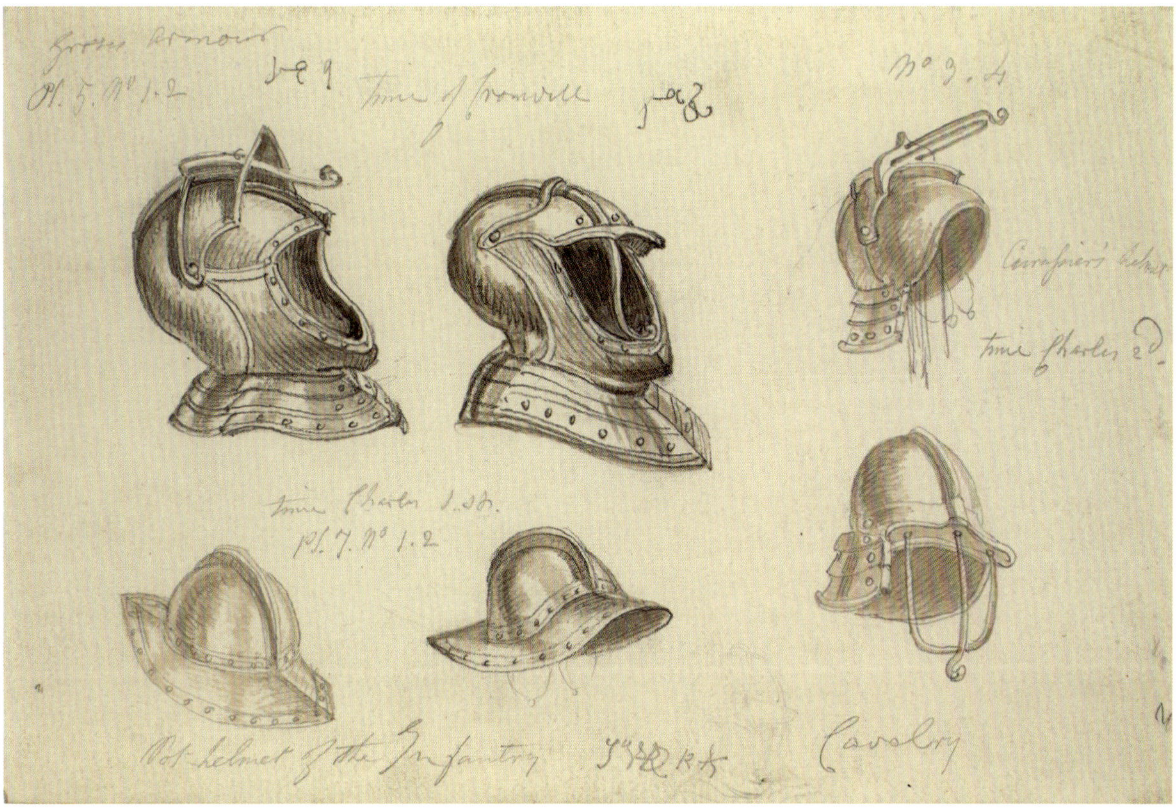
Gross Armour
time of Cromwell
time Charles I st
Pl. 7. N° 1. 2
Cuirassier's helmet
time Charles 2d
Pot helmet of the Infantry
Cavalry

69 STUDIES OF ARMOUR

Pencil and brown wash
7 × 10¼ inches · 178 × 260 mm
Signed *JWD RA*, dated 1824 and variously inscribed with notes: *Cromwell's time / Grosses [sic] armour / A bourgonet of the / time of Elizabelth / gorget of the time of Charles Ist / All this armour / is of the time of Charles I / with the / exception of / the helmet / which is a / bourgonet / of the time / of Elizabeth*

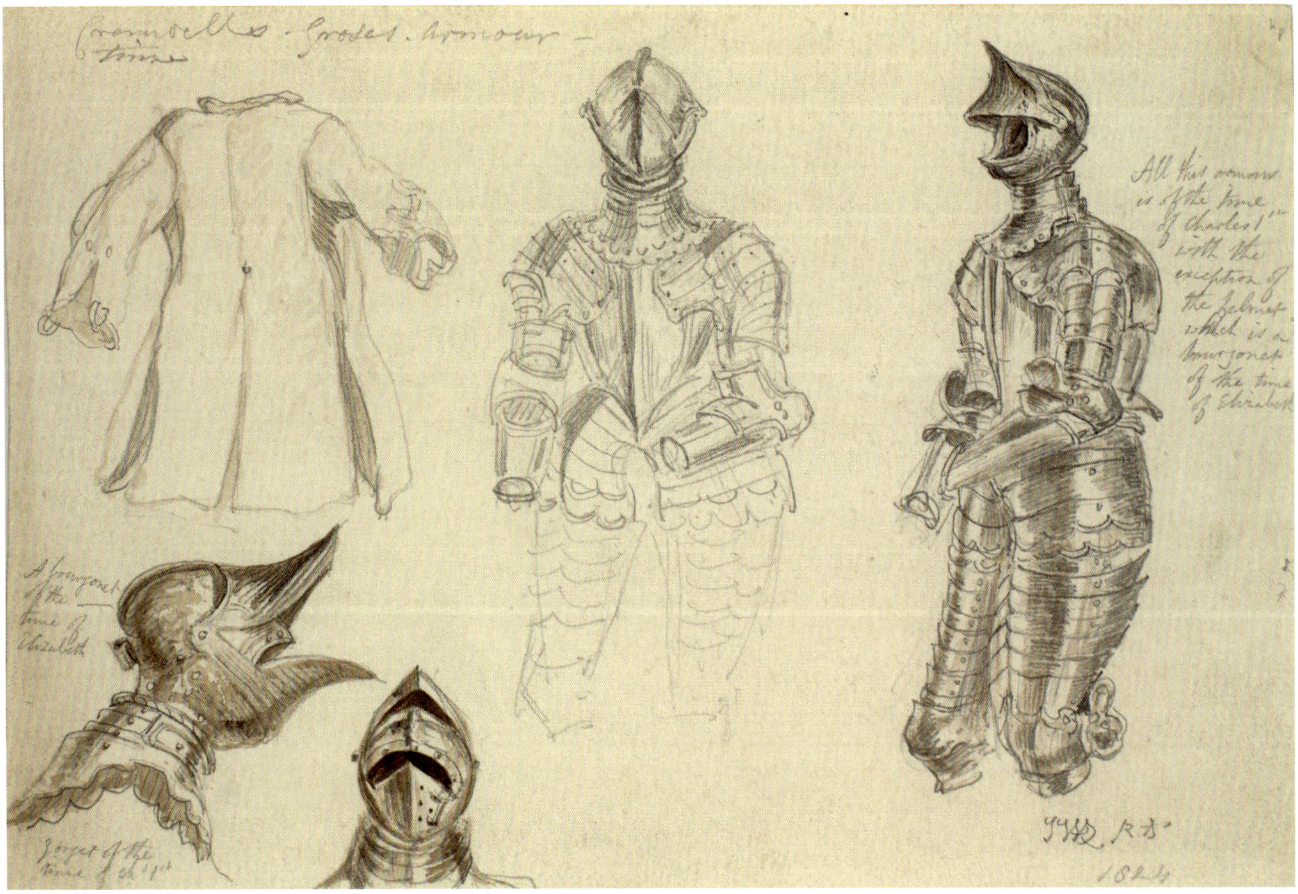

All of the studies on this sheet are based directly on various plates in Francis Grose's treatise. The coat on the left is the back view of the buff coat depicted in cat.67 is taken from and relates to plate 39, no.2. The two studies of armour relate to plates 45 and 46, no.1 respectively, and apparently depict a suit of armour which once belonged to the Duke of Monmouth.

70 STUDIES OF CROMWELLIAN BOOTS

Pencil and brown wash
7 × 10¼ inches · 178 × 260 mm
Signed *JWD RA*, dated 1824 and inscribed: *Boots in Cromwell's time / Haddon Hall 1824*

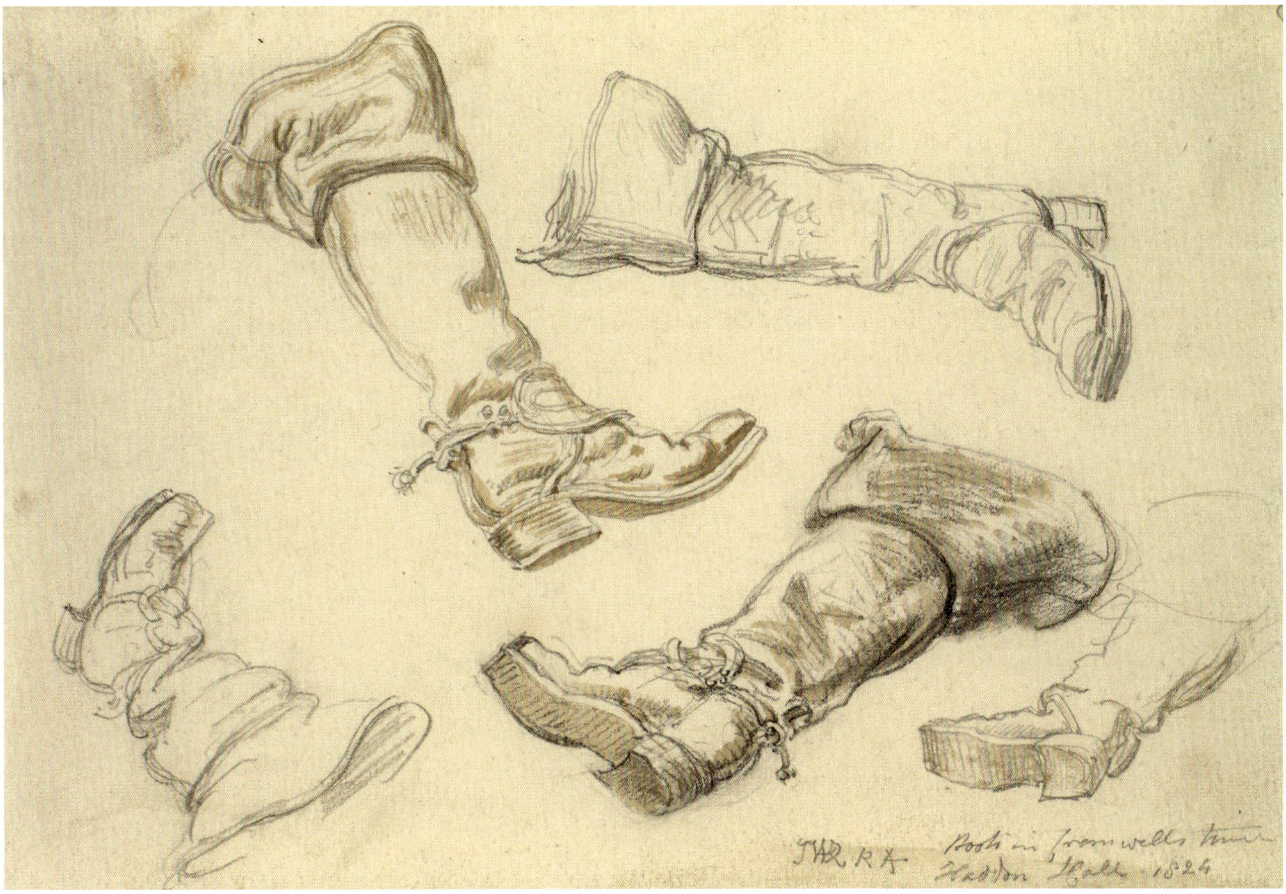

The inscription 'Haddon Hall' indicates that this sheet of studies was made whilst Ward was travelling in Derbyshire in 1824. Ward had a number of patrons in Derbyshire, including Philip Gell of Hopton Hall, where Ward made a detailed study of *Sir John Gell's Doublet* (cat.71) in January 1825. It seems likely that this study was made in December 1824 en route to stay with Gell.

71 SIR JOHN GELL'S DOUBLET

Pencil and watercolour
10¾ × 14¼ inches · 272 × 365 mm
Signed *JWD RA*, dated Jany 9 1825 and variously inscribed *Sir Gells Doublet / Weight above 15 lb* / Hopton, further inscribed in shorthand.

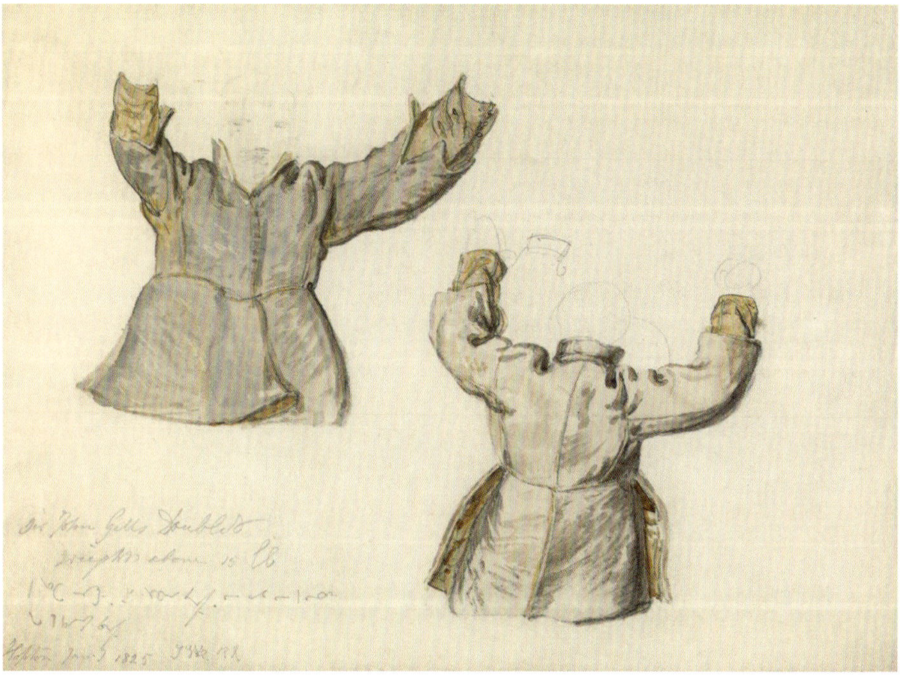

Ward visited Hopton in January 1825 whilst travelling through Derbyshire, where he had a number of friends, family and patrons. The Civil War commander Sir John Gell's descendant, Philip Gell, was a patron of Ward commissioning him to paint a portrait of his favourite pointer, Donald, which was exhibited at the Royal Academy in 1825 (collection, Boodle's, London)

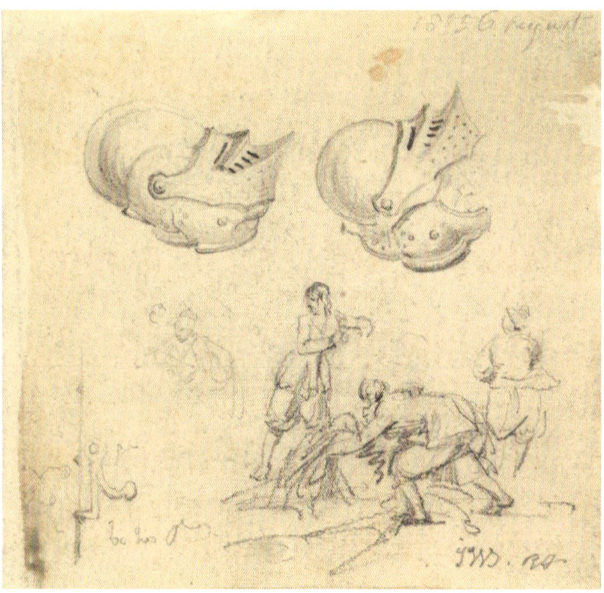

72 A SHEET WITH A GROUP OF FIGURES IN SEVENTEENTH CENTURY COSTUME AND STUDIES OF A HELMET

Pencil · 5¼ × 5½ inches · 133 × 140 mm
Signed *JWD RA* and dated August 1836

73 CORSELET, BESAGUES, VAMBRACE AND GAUNTLET

Pencil and watercolour
10¾ × 10⅜ inches · 271 × 264 mm
Signed *JWD RA* and inscribed in shorthand

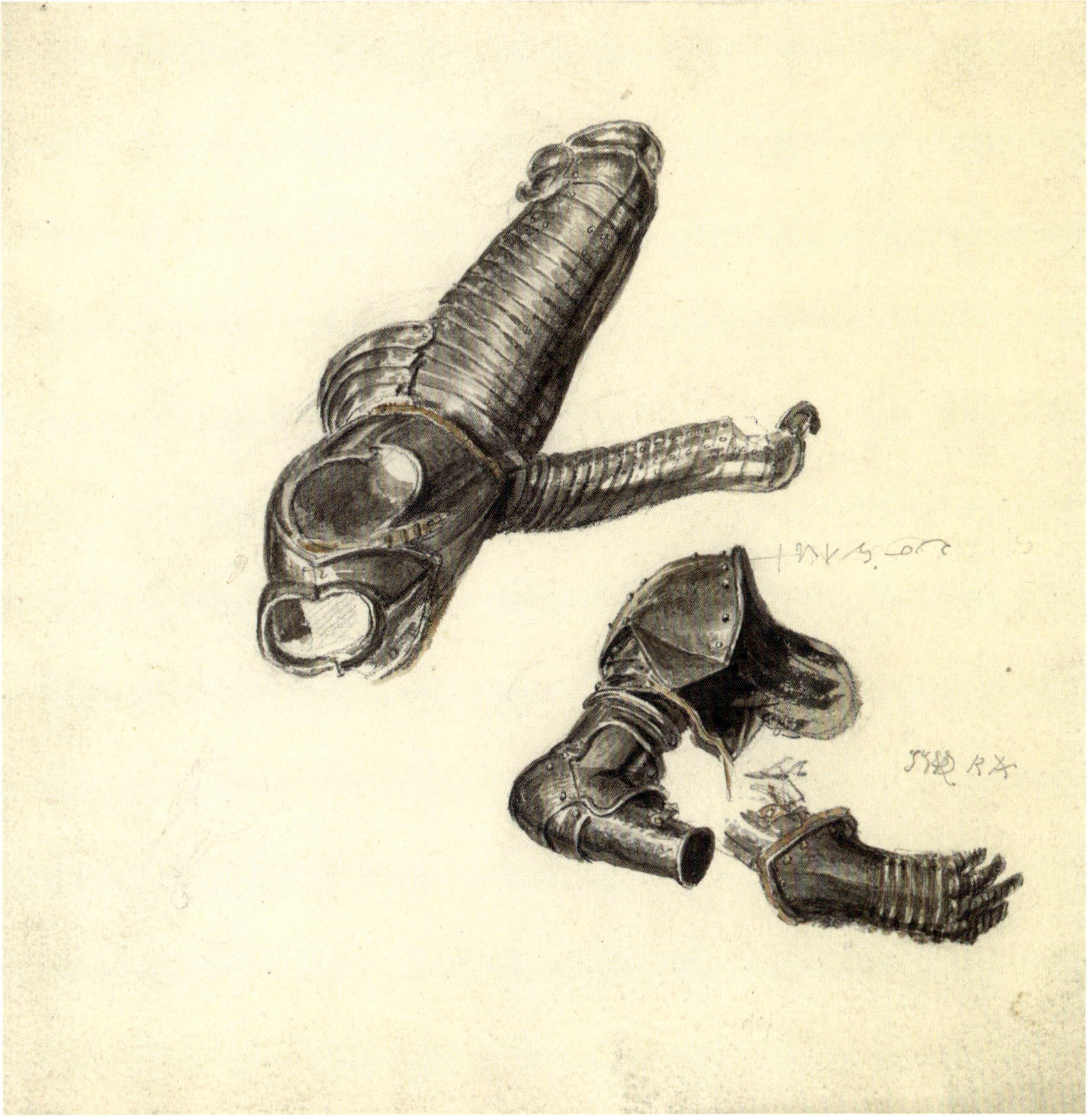

The present sheet with its clear emphasis on the interplay of light and shadow on the metalwork and in the careful articulation of the armour suggests that the studies were made from life, probably in preparation for the 1826 *Battle near Boston.*

74 STUDIES OF AN ENGLISH MATCHLOCK GUN

Pencil, watercolour and grey wash
5⅜ × 8⅝ inches · 137 × 219 mm
Signed JWD RA, inscribed *English Matchlock gun date 1640* and *5 feet 4&1 / 2 long* + *'The rest* +, further inscribed in shorthand.

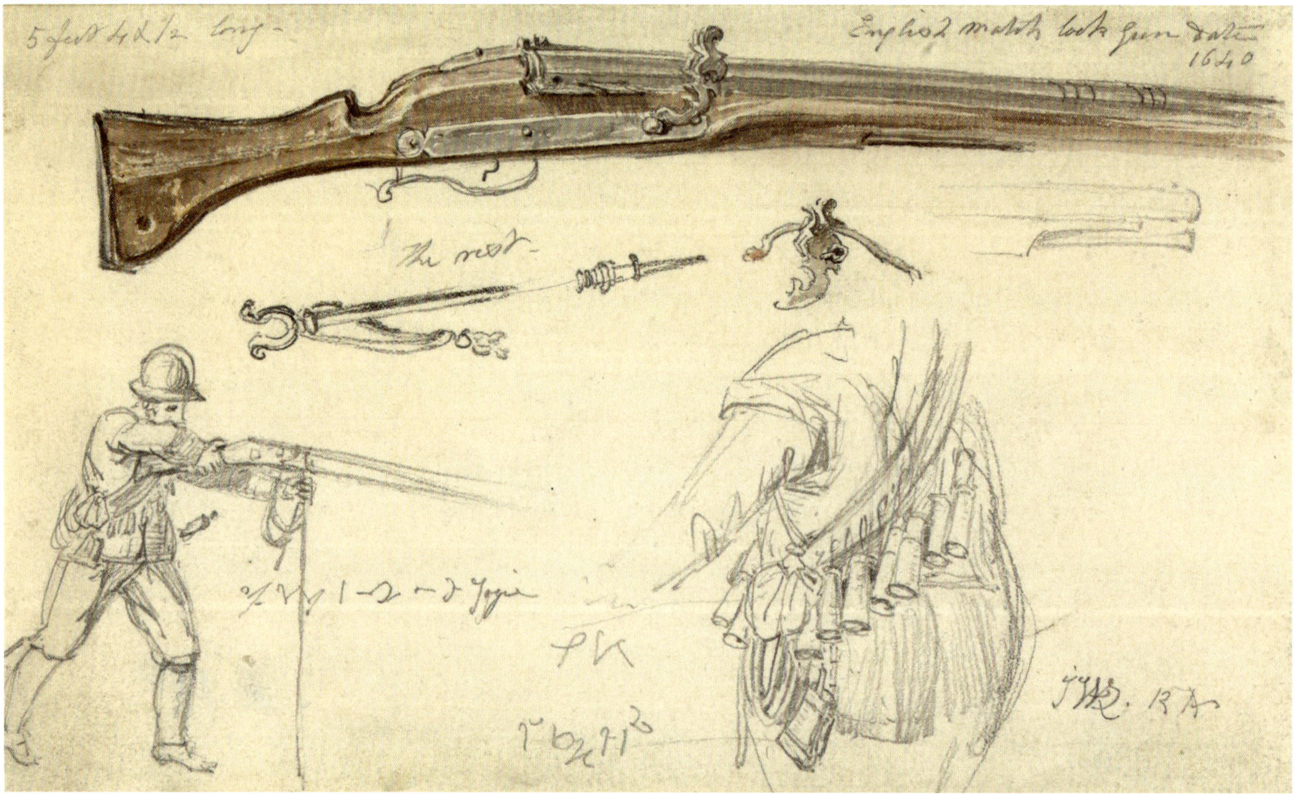

75 A ROYALIST AND REPUBLICAN SWORD HILTS

Pencil · 5½ × 8¾ inches · 140 × 222 mm
Signed *JWD RA* and inscribed *Royalist* and *Republican*, with the size of the swords noted and further inscribed in shorthand

75 B THREE REPUBLICAN SWORD HILTS AND A BLADE

Pencil · 5⅜ × 9 inches · 137 × 228 mm
Signed *JWD RA* and variously inscribed *Royalist* and *Republican / 2ft … / 2ft 6 In /* and further inscribed in shorthand

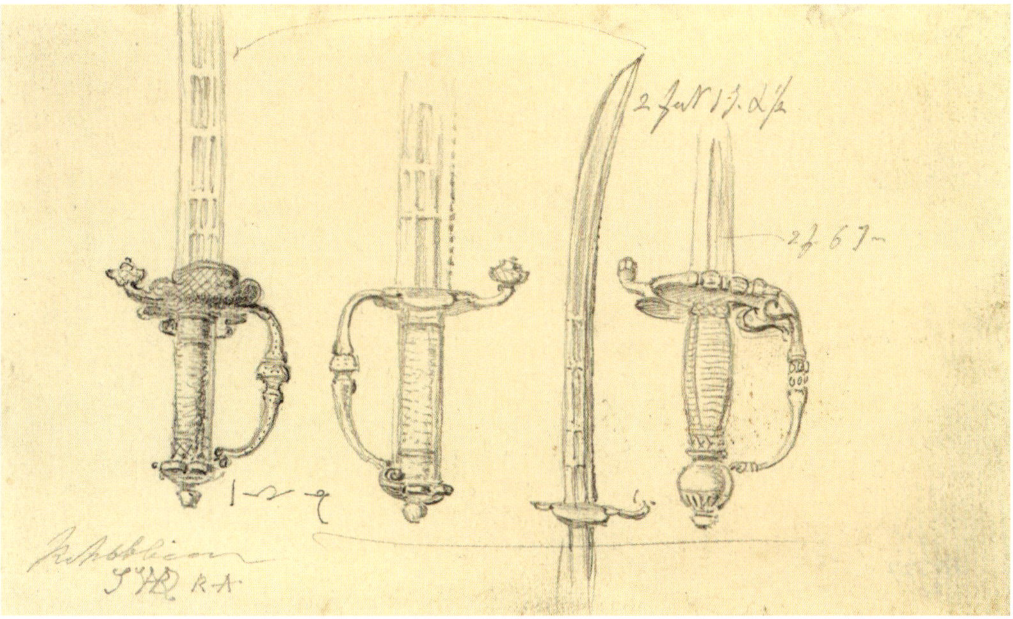

The inscription suggests that the artist had access to these weapons, perhaps through the antiquarian Sir Samuel Meyrick.

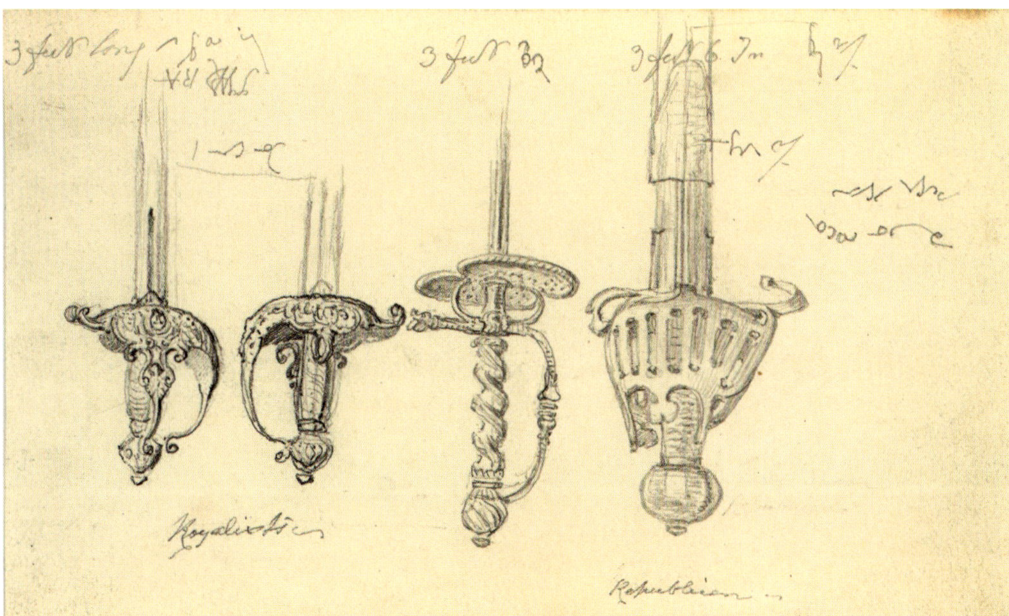

IV
Animals

Central to Ward's professional life was his interest in animals, and it is largely as an animal painter that he is remembered. Apart from the numerous private commissions to paint livestock, horses and dogs Ward also received commissions to record livestock on a national scale. Most significantly in 1800, Ward was commissioned by the Board of Agriculture and the print publisher Josiah Boydell to execute two hundred portraits of the finest examples of the various breeds of sheep, cattle and pigs in England, Scotland and Wales. The scheme was to be engraved by Boydell and Ward was to be paid 15 guineas per finished work. Boydell's bankruptcy put an end to the scheme and Ward was only paid a fraction of what he was expecting. Despite its failure, the scheme had an enormous impact on Ward's work. It introduced him to a group of wealthy potential patrons, who over the years commissioned many works from the artist. It also required him to travel extensively, introducing Ward to diverse landscapes and scenery.

Relatively early in his career, Ward established a reputation as a skilled artist of blood horses when his portrait of *Granadillo, a mare with her foal,* was exhibited at the Royal Academy in 1809 to great critical acclaim. Ward proved a highly perceptive observer of horses at both work and rest making him a popular painter in this genre. His abilities led to a commission to paint both Wellington's charger *Copenhage*n and Napoleon's *Marengo*, which had been sent to England following the Battle of Waterloo.

Ward's reputation as an animal painter was such that he proved influential to a number of French artists, such as Théodore Géricault and Eugène Delacroix and subsequently Alfred de Dreux and Jacques Brascassat, who looked towards Britain for inspiration. Géricault knew and admired Ward's work and may have met him when in London in the early 1820s when he was exhibiting the *Raft of the Medusa*.

76 A STUDY FOR 'VIRGIL'S BULLS'

Watercolour and pen and ink · 4¼ × 8 inches · 110 × 202 mm
Signed: *JWD RA*

COLLECTIONS: Mrs E L Evans; Anthony Reed

LITERATURE: Nygren, 1976, p.242, repr. fig. 262

The present highly realized watercolour was a study for *Virgil's Bulls*, exhibited at the Royal Academy in 1843 (no.9) and acquired by Charles Scarisbrick. Apparently there was once a note attached to this work with an inscription in the artist's hand which stated that it was *the first design for the picture of Virgil's Bulls.* The subject matter depicts an Alderney bull locking horns with a Chillingham bull and acts as a powerful example of Ward's enduring interest in breeds and the physiognomy of livestock. The subject matter relates to Ward's much earlier, highly successful painting, *Bulls fighting: A view of St Donat's Castle, Glamorganshire in the background* (Victoria and Albert Museum, London). *Bulls Fighting* was painted in response to Rubens' *Chateau de Steen* and was much admired by contemporaries. In April 1857, Ward wrote to his son George recounting Benjamin West's comments on seeing *Bulls Fighting.* Apparently West considered this as 'the perfection of execution, and when I … look at the Rubens I find it to be gross and vulgar' (Nygren, 2013, p.244). This admiration was also to be found in 1843 when the oil of *Virgil's Bulls* (location unknown) was described in the handbook to the exhibition: this is not a jejune and meagre commentory on the text; it tells the fierce and furied conflict in all the verities of jealousy and rage and monster – vigour and energy. Mr Ward has exhausted a just feeling in his selection of the scene of this dark and fearful conflict; the heavens lower around and earth trembles. His manner is bold and daring; the result of unlimited confidence in his power over art.

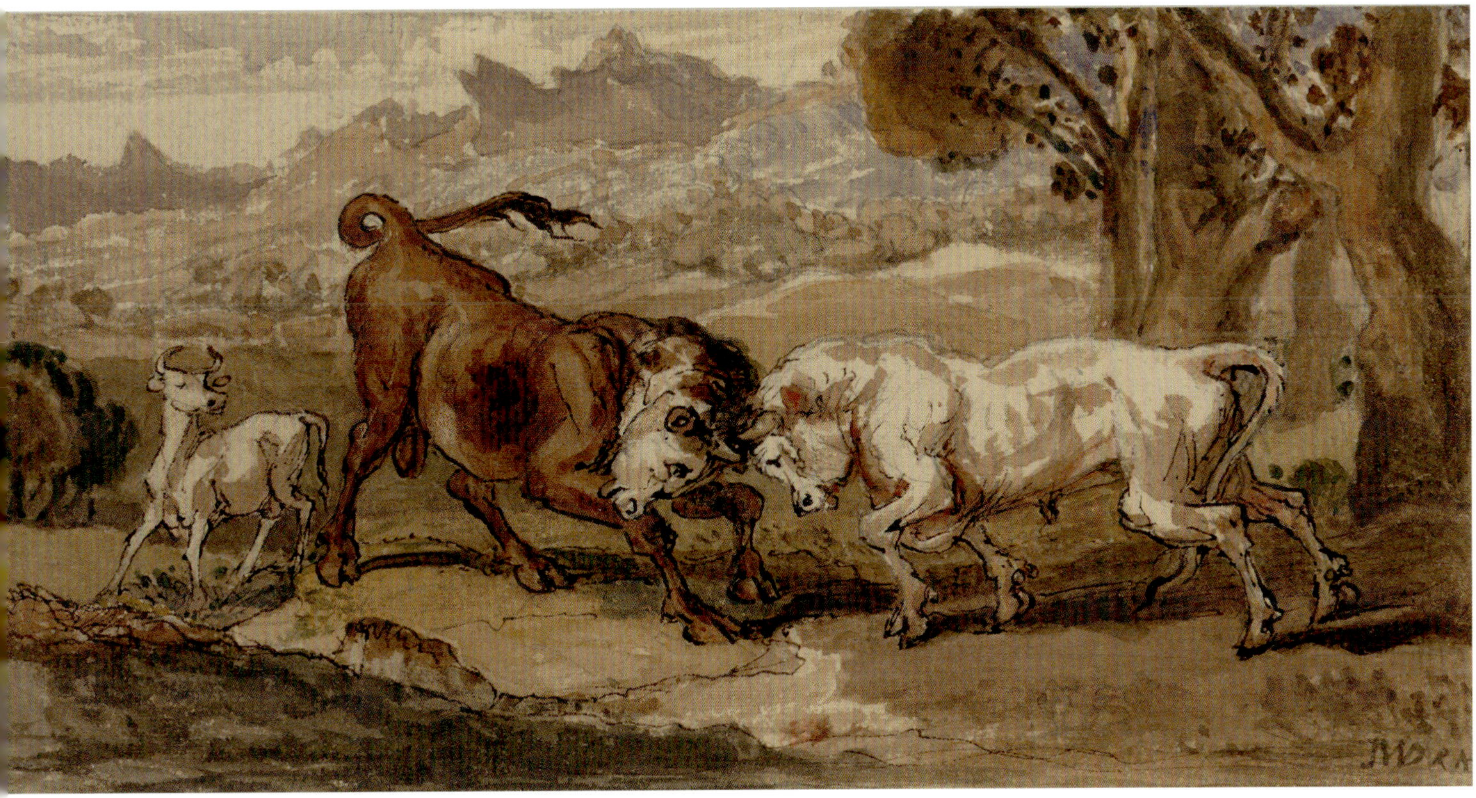

77 STUDIES OF CATTLE WATERING

£6,000

Oil on paper · 3 × 12 inches · 99 × 321 mm
Signed *JWD RA*

COLLECTIONS: Knowles of Hanwell by 1951; Prudence Summerhayes (a descendant of Ward) by 1959; by descent to 2008.

EXHIBITED: London, W.S. Fine Art Ltd, *Drawings by James Ward 1769–1859*, 2009, cat.65

@ £850

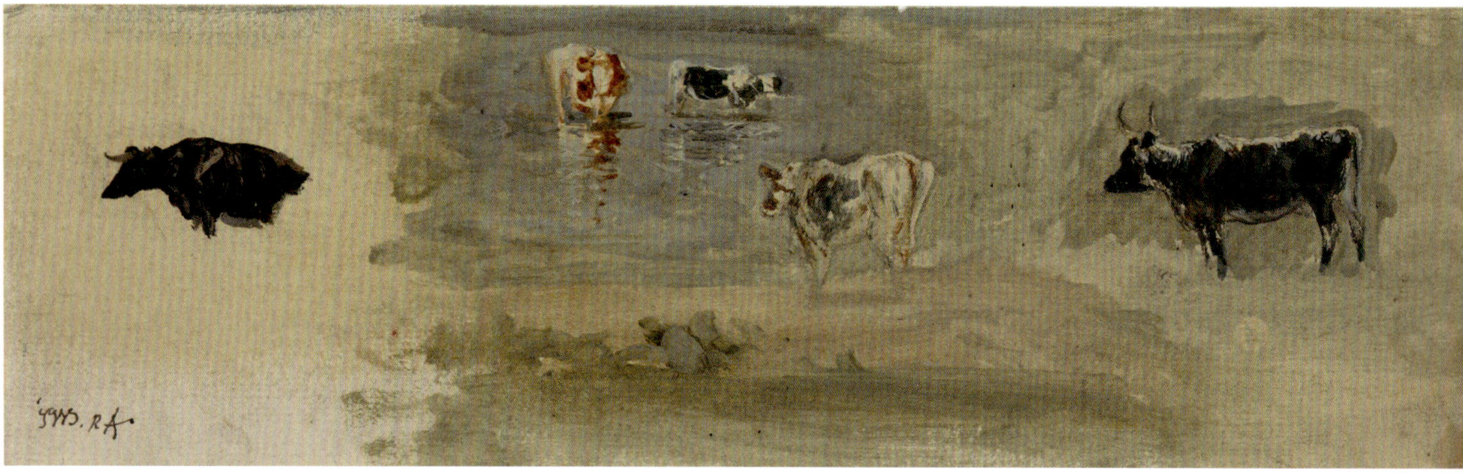

78 A SHORTHORN HEIFER

Oil over pencil on artist's board
9½ × 13 inches · 241 × 330 mm
Provenance:
Mrs E. M. Ward, 1924

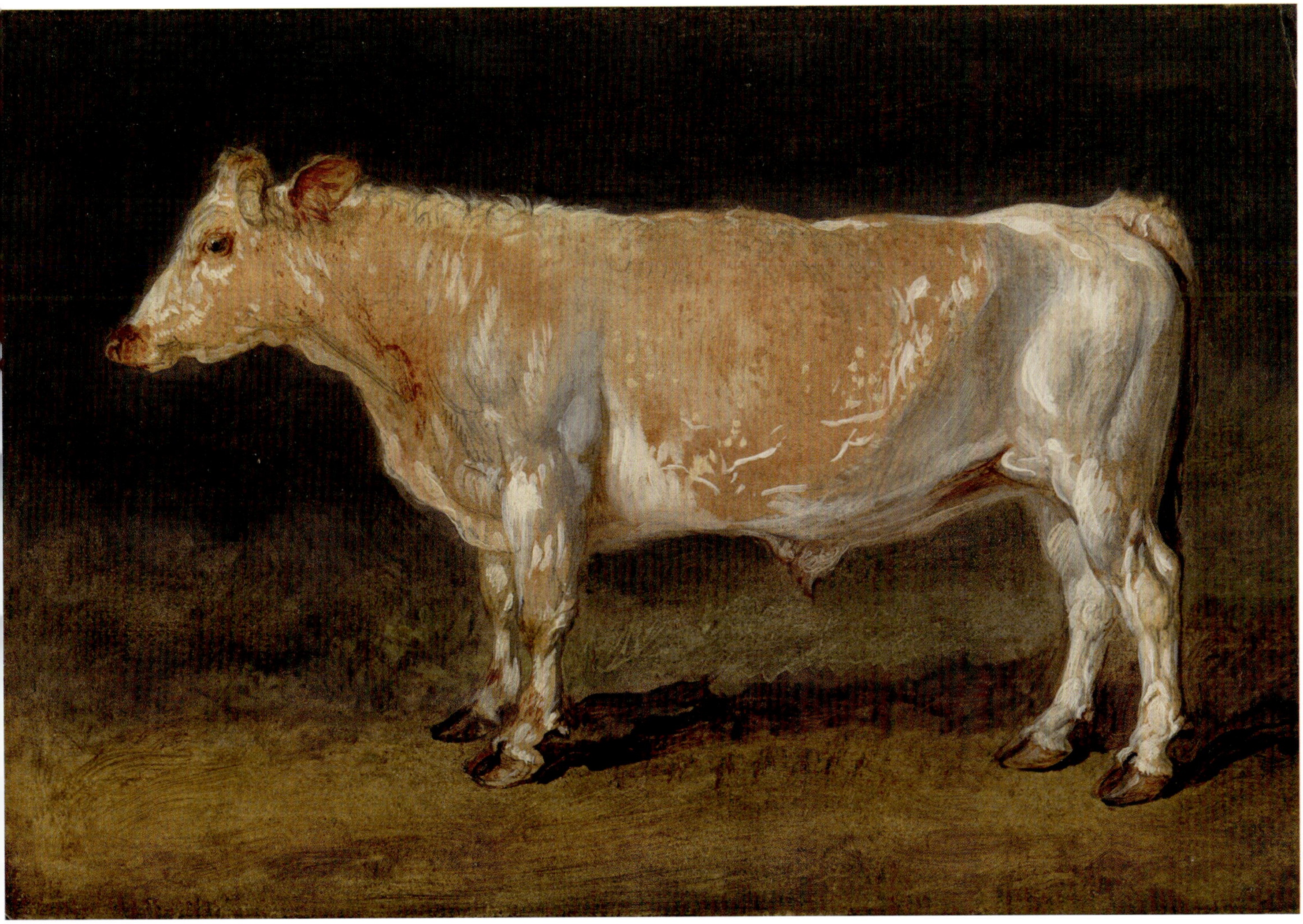

The present oil study is typical of the sort of work that Ward produced as a record of livestock for The Board of Agriculture. The lack of detailed background emphasises that the subject is all important.

79 A SHEEP AND LAMB

Pencil · 5½ × 5⅝ inches · 140 × 143 mm

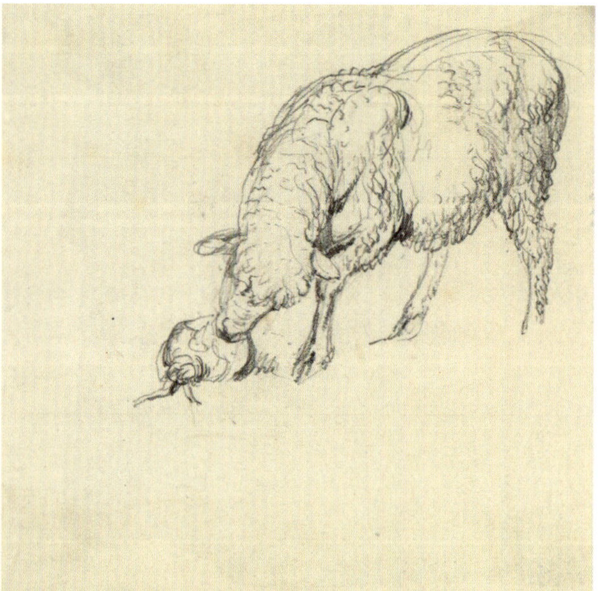

80 A SHEEP AND A SHORN FLEECE

Oil on canvas · 10⅛ × 13¼ inches · 259 × 336 mm
Signed *JWD RA* and also with IWRA branded onto the stretcher

LITERATURE: Basil Taylor, *Animal painting in England*, 1955, p.66 repr. in colour pl.IV

EXHIBITED: London, Plymouth, Newcastle-upon-Tyne, Leeds & Cardiff, Arts Council exhibition, *James Ward 1769–1859*, 1960, no.52.

Although an unusual subject for most artists, this painting of a sheared sheep demonstrates Ward's fascination with agricultural activities. The present work appears to be closely related to *Sheep-shearing: Taking off their clothes* (Nygren, 2013, p.365) which Ward exhibited at the Royal Academy in 1846 (354).

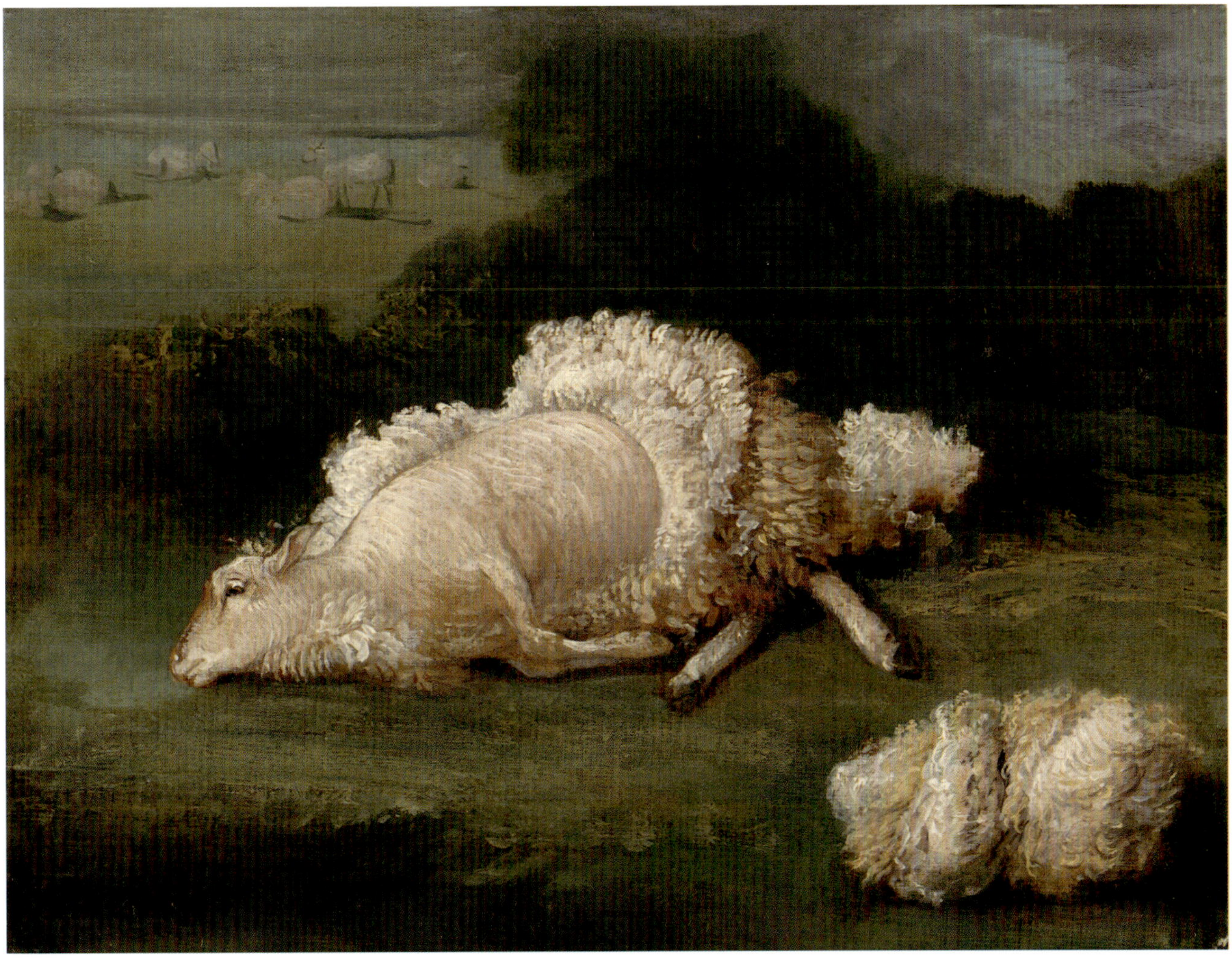

81 A STUDY OF A DONKEY AND HER FOAL

Watercolour · 7 × 5⅞ inches · 178 × 148 mm

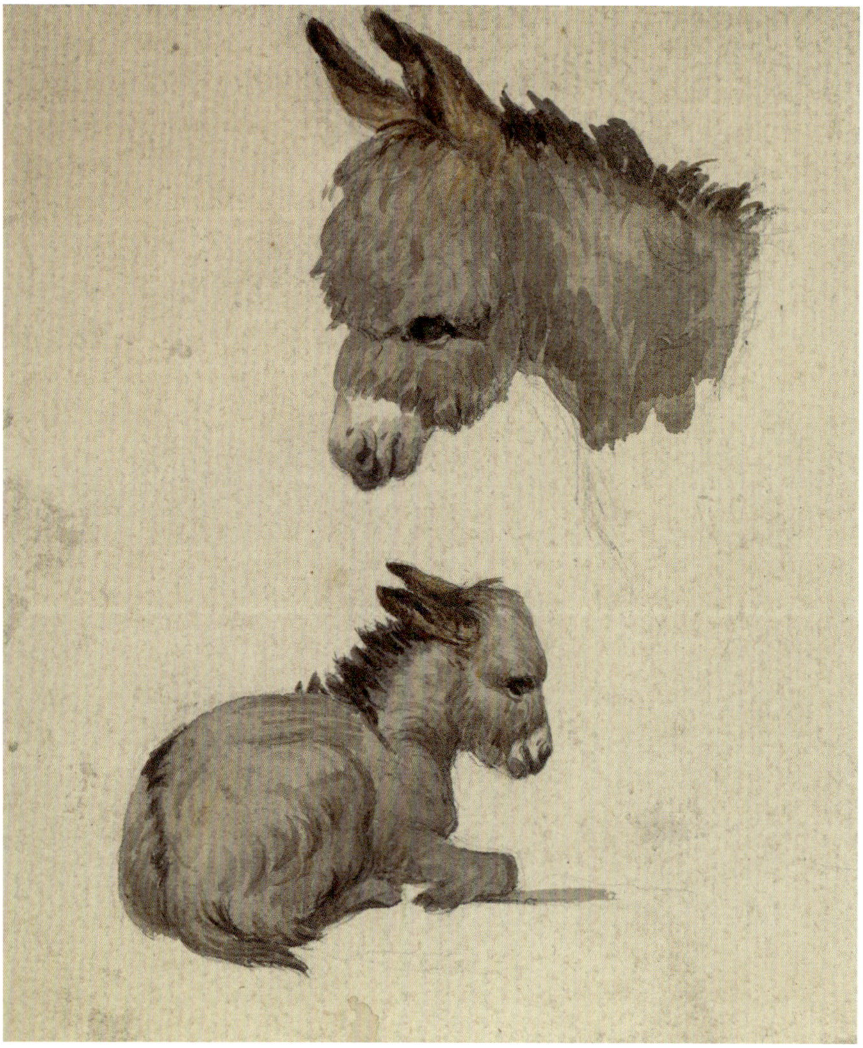

This attractive watercolour study is similar to a sheet of studies of a donkey and foal in the Fitzwilliam Museum, Cambridge.

82 THE HINDQUARTERS OF A HORSE

Pencil · 6¼ × 4¾ inches · 158 × 120 mm
Signed: *JW*

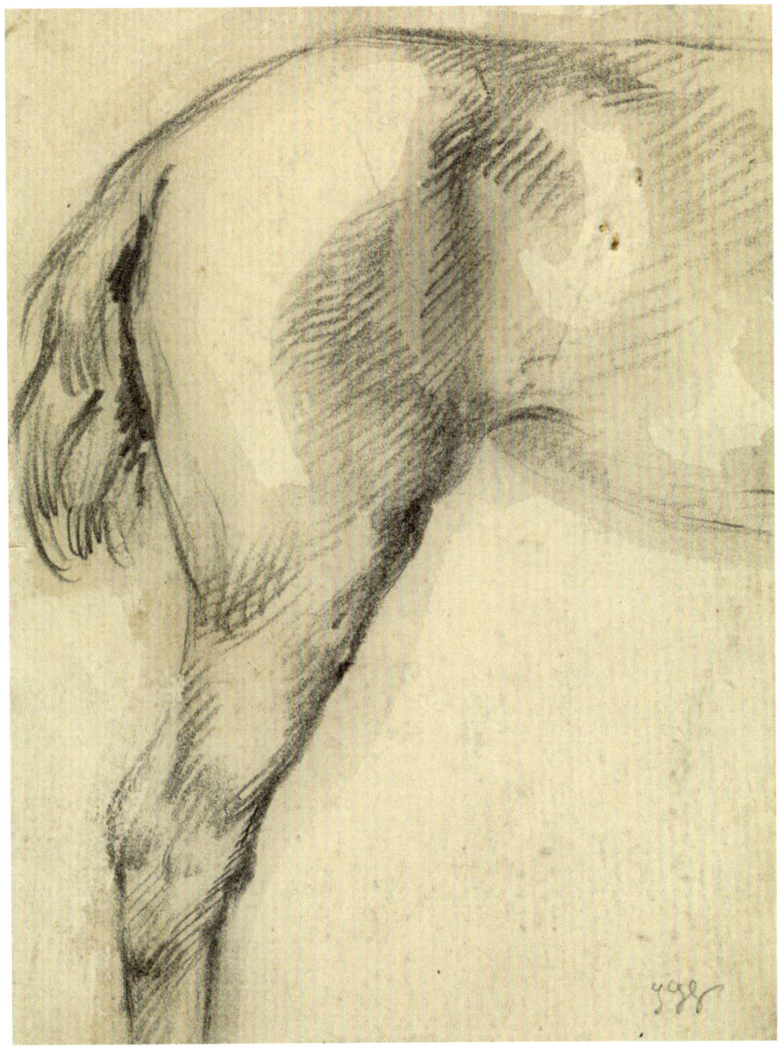

This careful study of the hindquarters of a horse demonstrates Ward's meticulous study of subjects that interested him. He had an extraordinary understanding of horses – their anatomy, the way they stood and moved – and it was through careful studies, such as the present example, that much of this understanding would have derived.

83 STUDIES OF HORSES

Pencil · 7½ × 9¾ inches · 190 × 248 mm
Signed: *JWD RA*

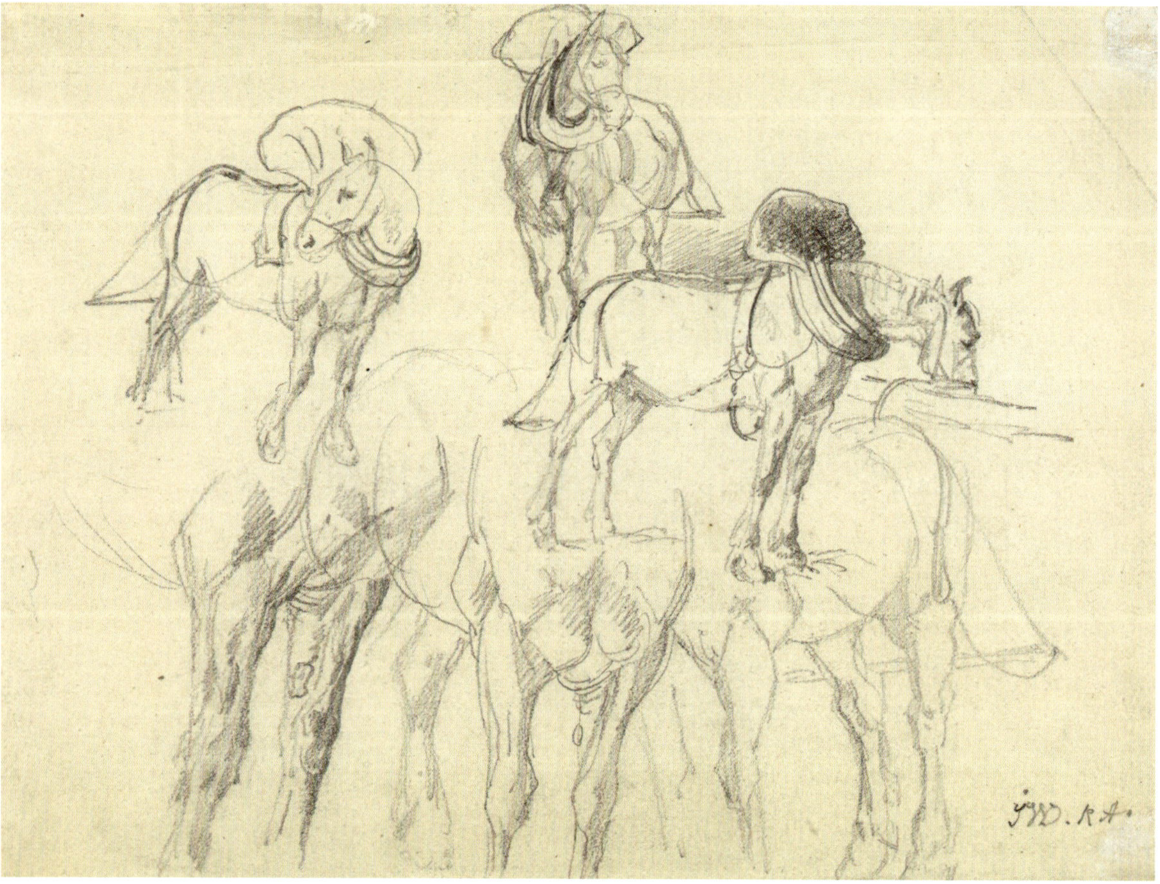

This sheet combines rapid sketches of working horses still in harness with more detailed anatomical studies. The interplay of figures creates a sense of movement and dynamism, which makes these studies particularly appealing. The present sheet recalls the work of Théodore Géricault who, like many of his contemporaries including Delacroix, was influenced by the work of Ward.

84 A STUDY OF HORSES

Pencil · 7 × 10¼ inches · 178 × 260 mm
Signed: *JWD RA*

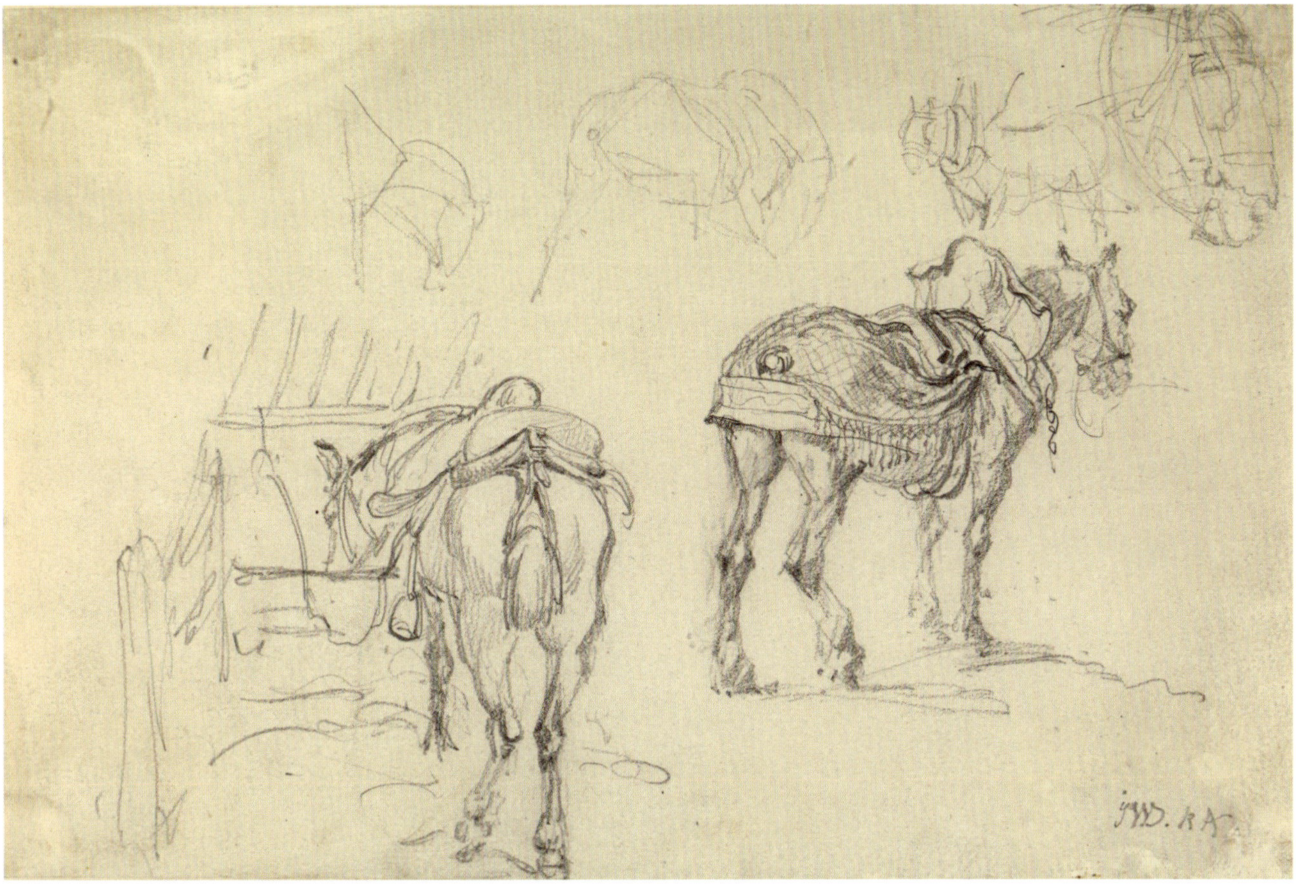

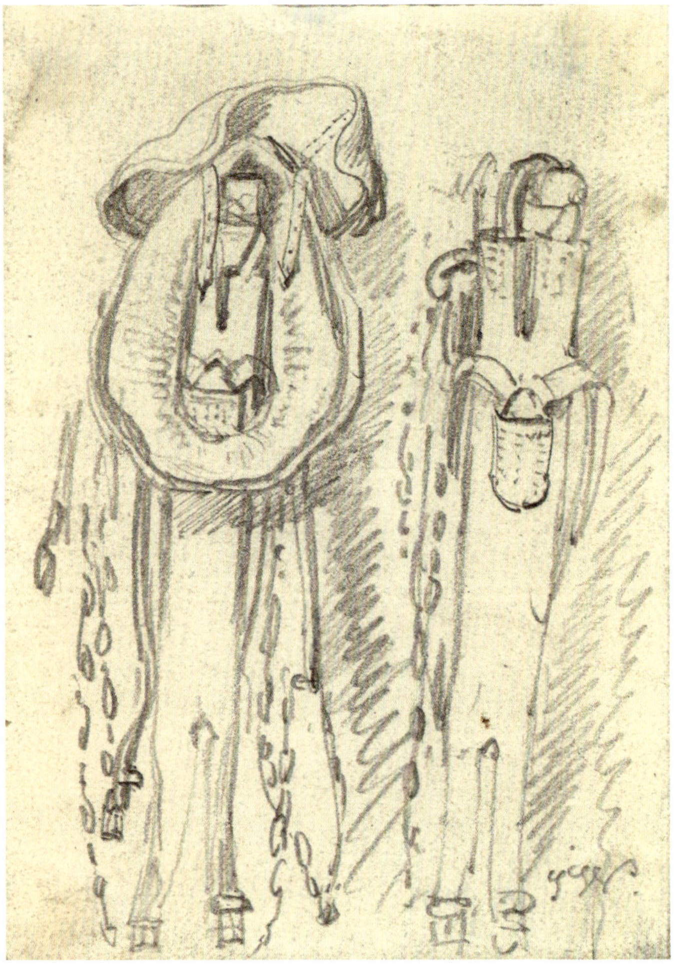

85 PLOUGHING HARNESS: HORSE COLLAR AND BELLY BAND

Pencil · 4¾ × 3½ inches · 120 × 88 mm
Signed: *JW*

86 A STUDY OF PIGS

Pencil
6¼ × 10 inches · 160 × 254 mm
Signed: *JW*
Slight sketch *verso* of the lower part of figure

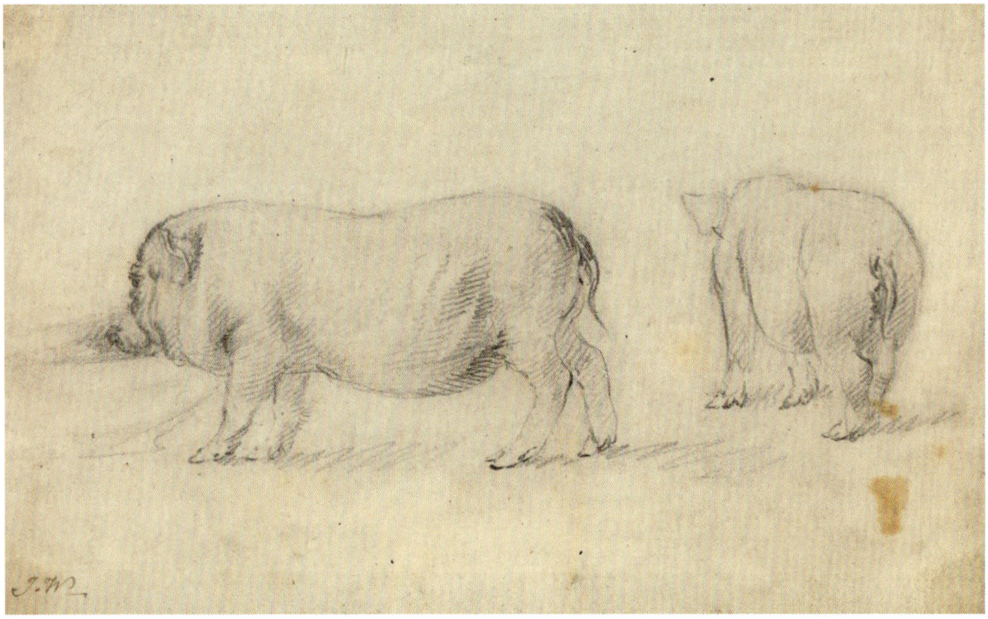

87 ANNETTE, A SCOTCH TERRIER

Pencil on laid paper · 7½ × 6¼ inches · 190 × 159 mm
Signed: *JW*

EXHIBITED: London, Plymouth, Newcastle-upon-Tyne, Leeds & Cardiff, Arts Council exhibition, *James Ward 1769–1859*, 1960, no.66

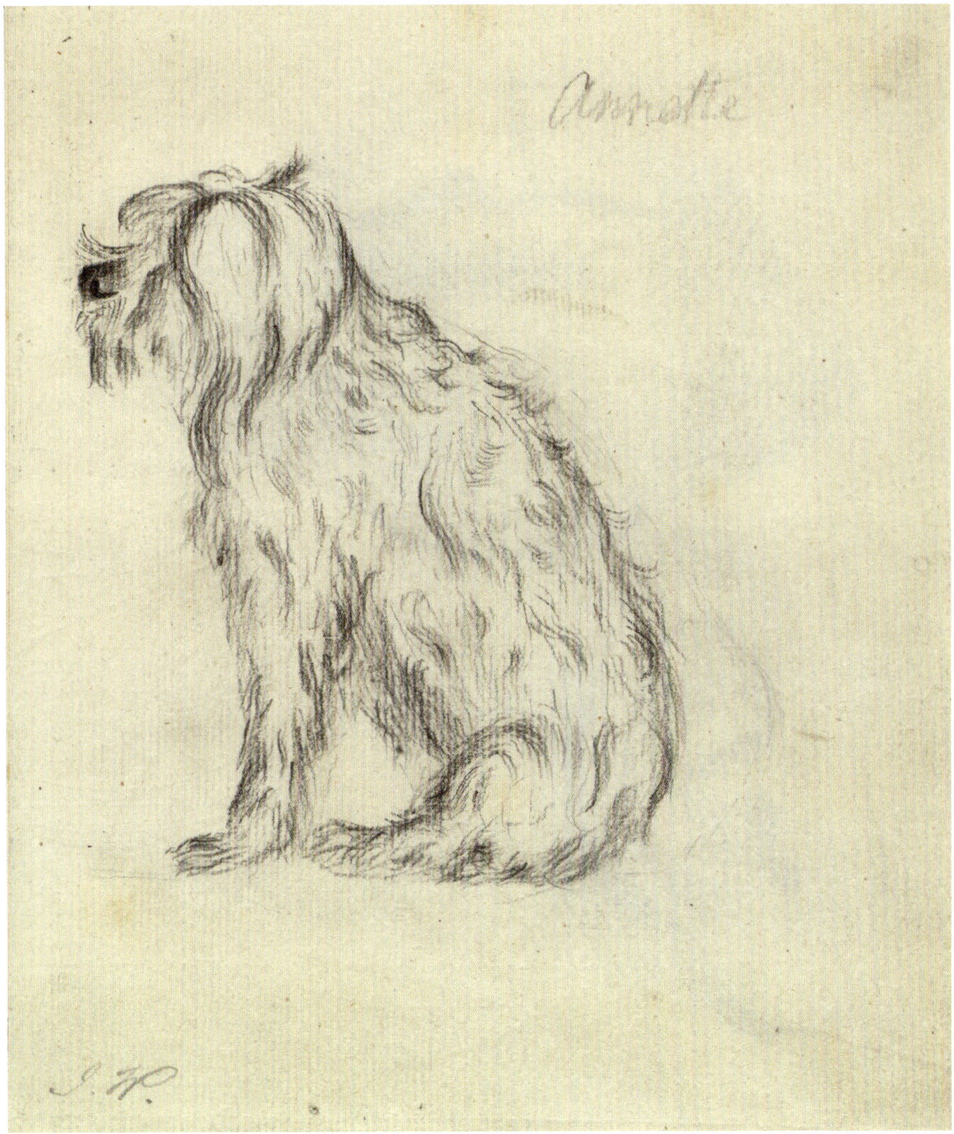

Ward exhibited a number of paintings of dogs, including various terriers. *Vixen* was exhibited at the Royal Academy in 1807 (no.607) and *Sir A Hume's Terrier*, four years later, also at the Royal Academy (no.40).

Catalogue Notes

SIGNATURES

Around 1844, perhaps in anticipation of selling his entire stock of paintings, drawings and sketches to the dealer Thomas Griffith in return for an annuity, Ward went through his drawings signing them *JWD RA* or a compacted form of *JWARD RA*. The rapidity of this process resulted in some drawings which ended up being signed twice or the wrong way around. Earlier forms of his signature are the initials *JW* or *JWD*. Ward took to branding the back of panels or stretchers with the device *IW* or *IWRA* to prevent unscrupulous dealers from changing the attribution of his works to that of his brother-in-law, George Morland.

SHORTHAND

The shorthand used by Ward is a standard eighteenth century 'Natural Shorthand' invented by William Holdsworth and William Aldridge who both worked for the Bank of England. This system – one of many shorthand systems used in the eighteenth and nineteenth centuries – was first published in 1766 as *Natural Shorthand, wherein the nature of speech and the manner of pronunciation are briefly explained.* It was also used by the watercolourist Robert Hills who also specialised in animals and landscapes.

Acknowledgements

This catalogue and exhibition are the result of much hard work on the part of many. I am grateful to Sarah Hobrough who took on the main task of collating and researching this substantial group of Ward's work and to Helen Libson who has, at a late stage, undertaken the role of organizing and co-ordinating this project. I am also very appreciative of Deborah Greenhalgh and Jonny Yarker for well-judged advice and editorial skills as well as to Laurence Allan for keeping track (for most of the time) of so many unframed drawings and for his usual talent for framing, mounting and presenting these works by Ward to advantage. I also owe thanks to Loyd Grossman who was enthusiastic enough to find time aside of his numerous activities to write the foreword for our catalogue. Loyd is currently working on Benjamin West, Ward's good friend and close neighbour, and it is appropriate that these two ambitious artists should once again be linked.

The majority of the works included in this catalogue had been assembled over many years by the highly respected collector and dealer Peter Cochrane (1913–2004), whilst a number have come from other sources including the Ingram and Reed collections.

Anyone working on Ward for the last forty or so years owes a huge debt to Anthony Reed for his unfailing championship of this fine artist as well as to Edward J. Nygren for his long standing dedication to Ward. I am particularly indebted to Ed for his many pertinent comments on our catalogue entries which have saved us from a number of inaccuracies and infelicities; any faults remaining are entirely our own. It is fortuitous that this catalogue appears at the same moment that Ed's important monograph *James Ward, RA (1769–1859): Papers and Patrons* is published by the Walpole Society. This modest catalogue is dedicated to these two important Ward stalwarts.

LOWELL LIBSON

Chronology & Travels

Throughout his long career Ward travelled frequently and extensively in Britain, however there are no detailed records of these. His journeys around the country are mainly known through notes in his account books, his letters and through dates and inscriptions on his drawings. He spent virtually every summer on the road; travelling the length and breadth of the country he made extended stays in Kent, Hampshire, Dorset, Wiltshire, the West Country, the Midlands, East Anglia, Cheshire, Yorkshire, Northumberland and Scotland. Like many of his contemporaries he also managed to make a three month continental trip to Paris.

1769 Born in London, 23 October

1781/2 Embarked on career as a print maker. Apprenticed to John Raphael Smith (1752–1812)

1783 Became apprenticed to his brother William (1766–1828)

1791 Completed apprenticeship to his brother and embarked on career as an engraver

1792 First independent plates published by T. Simpson

1794 Appointed Engraver in Mezzotint to HRH the Prince of Wales

1794 Married Mary Ann Ward, 4 December

1797 Applied, unsuccessfully, for a place at the Royal Academy Schools

1798 James and William Ward set up as print publishers with Dr William Daw

1799 Announces intention to abandon practice as an engraver and take up painting

1799 Visits: Isle of Wight

*c.***1800** First major commission from the Board of Agriculture and Boydell, the print-publisher, to record the best examples of the various breeds of livestock

1801 Attended anatomy lectures held by Joshua Brookes and performed dissections of men and beasts

1802 Visits: Wales, Gloucestershire and Herefordshire

1805 Visits: Scotland

1807 Failure of the Boydell/Board of Agriculture scheme

1807 Elected an Associate of the Royal Academy

1807 Second visit to Wales. Also spent time in Wiltshire, apparently at the invitation of Thomas Crook of Tytherton

1809 First portrait of a pure breed horse exhibited at the Royal Academy: *Granadillo, a mare with her foal*

1811 Elected full Royal Academician

1811 Visits: (summer) Wiltshire and Dorset before heading north to Yorkshire, via the Malvern Hills, Gloucestershire, Manchester and Blackburn amongst others

1811 Visits Gordale Scar, began to formulate probably his most important painting, of Gordale Scar, commissioned by Lord Ribblesdale

1811 Visits: Staffordshire and Derbyshire (during the Autumn)

1815–20 Worked on the *Allegory of the Battle of Waterloo*

1817 November, death of favourite daughter, Emma

1818 Visits: Margate

1819 Visits: Northumberland

1819 September, death of first wife, Mary Ann

1820 Visits: Derbyshire and the Trent Valley

1821 Visits: Dorset, South Wiltshire

1821 Death of youngest son, Somerville

1821 The *Waterloo Allegory* exhibited

1822 Visits: Northamptonshire

1822 Visits: Wiltshire

1824 Visits: Newmarket, Staffordshire, Wales (Sir Thomas Mostyn), Cheshire (Tabley Park)

1824 Began to work on his Civil War paintings

1825 Visits: Derbyshire

1825 Three month stay in Paris

1826 Visits: Cheshire, Staffordshire, Northamptonshire and Wiltshire

1827 Marries second wife, Charlotte Fritche

1829 Sale of Ward's work at Christie's (29 May)

1830 Moved to Round Croft Cottage, Cheshunt, Hertfordshire, where he remained until his death

1833 East Anglian tour, Essex, Suffolk and Norfolk (in connection with the Myers Agricultural scheme)

1835 Sale of Ward's works at Phillips (4 March)

1850s Visits: Kent, Ramsgate

1855 Last painting exhibited at Royal Academy, *Morning Grey*

1855 Suffered stroke which left him paralysed down one side and unable to work

1859 Died at Cheshunt, 16 November

Select Bibliography

JAMES WARD, *Some Account of Mary Thomas of Tanyralt in Merionethshire, who has existed many Years without Taking Food; and of Ann Moore, commonly called the fasting Woman of Tutbury, accompanied with Portraits and Illustrative Etchings*, 1813

JAMES WARD, *An Explanatory Description of the Battle of Waterloo in an Allegory Painted for the Directors of the British Institution … now Exhibiting at the Egyptian Hall, Piccadilly, with moral Reflections*, 1821

JAMES WARD, *A Descriptive Catalogue of Pictures painted by James Ward, Esq.* RA *now exhibiting at No. 6 Newman Street*, 1822

ANONYMOUS, 'James Ward, RA', *The Sporting Magazine*, XIX N.S., November and December 1826, pp.1–3, 102–03

JAMES WARD, *Description of Ward's Gallery of Paintings*, 1841

JAMES WARD, *A Defence of the Beard, c.* 1849

JAMES WARD, 'Memoirs of James Ward RA', *The Art-Journal*, xi, 1849, 179–81

'OBITUARY: JAMES WARD RA', *The Art-Journal*, xxii, 1860, p. 9

JAMES DAFFORNE, 'British Artists: James Ward', *The Art Journal*, 1862, pp.169–71

G.G. STEPHENS,'James Ward', *The Portfolio*, 17, 1886, pp.8–14, 32–36, 45–48

ERNEST FLETCHER ED., *Conversations of James Nothcote R.A with James Ward on Art and Artists*, London 1901

JULIA FRANKAU, *William Ward* ARA, *James Ward* RA: *Their Lives and Works*, 1904

GRUNDY AND ROBINSON'S, Mount Street, *Catalogue of an Exhibition of Pictures and Sketches, by James Ward* RA, June 1907

C. REGINALD GRUNDY, *James Ward* RA: *His Life and Works*, 1909

WALTER SHAW SPARROW, 'The Versatility of James Ward RA', *Connoisseur*, 97, 1936, pp.3–8

WALTER SHAW SPARROW, 'A Few Words on James Ward RA', *Country Life*, 79, 1936, pp.18–19

GEOFFREY GRIGSON, 'James Ward Reconsidered', *Country Life*, 107, 1950, pp.97–98

PRUDENCE SUMMERHAYES, 'An Artist's Account Book', *Connoisseur Year Book*, 1959, pp.52–57

PRUDENCE SUMMERHAYES, 'James Ward', *The Countryman*, 56, 1959, pp.91–99

DENNIS FARR, *James Ward 1769–1859*, 1960, exhibition catalogue

DENYS SUTTON, 'The Curious and Tragic James Ward', *Country Life*, 127, 1960, pp.60–61

'DAGENHAM: ECONOMIC HISTORY AND LOCAL GOVERNMENT', *A History of the County of Essex: Volume 5*, 1966

PRUDENCE SUMMERHAYES, 'James Ward and His Dogs', *Country Life*, 151, 1972, pp.322–24

OLIVER BECKETT, 'James Ward RA: An Under-Rated Genius', *Stud & Stable*, 12 (October 1973), pp.66–71

G.E. FUSSELL, *James Ward* RA: *Animal Painter 1769–1859 and his England*, 1974

EDWARD J. NYGREN, *The Art of James Ward* RA *(1769–1859)*, unpublished doctoral thesis, Yale, 1976

PRUDENCE SUMMERHAYES, 'Great Picture in Obscurity: James Ward RA and Gordale Scar', *Country Life*, 162, 1977, pp.154–55

JUDY EGERTON, *British Sporting and Animal Paintings 1655–1867: The Paul Mellon Collection*, 1978

JUDY EGERTON, *British Sporting and Animal Drawings, c.1500–1850*, 1978

EDWARD J. NYGREN, 'James Ward's Exhibition Pictures of 1838: Controversy in Paint', *The Art Bulletin*, lxi.3, September 1979, pp.448–59

PRUDENCE SUMMERHAYES, 'Hetman of the Cossacks: Count Platov (1751–1818)', *Country Life*, 171, 1982, pp.156–58

EDWARD J. NYGREN, *James Ward's 'Gordale Scar': An Essay in the Sublime*, 1983, exhibition catalogue

JANE MUNRO, *James Ward RA 1769–1859*, 1991, exhibition catalogue

OLIVER BECKETT, *The Life and Work of James Ward RA 1769–1859: The Forgotten Genius*, 1995

MALCOLM WARNER, *James Ward, The Day's Sport, 1826: Paintings from the Yale Center for British Art*, 1998, exhibition catalogue

EDWARD J. NYGREN, *James Ward and Drawing: A Sesquicentennial Tribute, Drawings by James Ward 1769–1859 on the Occasion of the 150th Anniversary of the Artist's Death*, 2009, exhibition catalogue

EDWARD J. NYGREN, 'James Ward's Papers: An 1826 Diary in Context', *Getty Research Journal*, 3, 2011, pp.179–88

EDWARD J. NYGREN, 'James Ward RA (1769–1859): Papers and Patrons', The Walpole Society, vol.LXXV, 2013